Practicing the Sabbath with Community

Daniel Goldstein

Jewels of Judaism Publishing
Jerusalem, Israel

JewelsofJudaism@gmail.com

Edited by Rittie Katz

Cover design by Chuck Dillon

ISBN: 978-965-91717-1-2

First Printing: July 2011

Printed in Jerusalem, Israel

For more information about this book or other Jewish resources contact:

JewelsofJudaism@gmail.com

This book is dedicated to my grandparents
Samuel & Ruth Goldstein
whose lives were preserved during the holocaust
and have given to me my Jewish identity.

Acknowledgments

This book was written over the period of three years and during this time I asked many friends and family members to read the manuscript and give me their thoughts. If I listed each person there would probably be a book full of names. In lieu of this, I'd like to thank each person that has contributed to this book. I never could have achieved this without the help of each one.

Contents

Introduction

I was raised in a typical American home. My mother's ancestors are Jews who immigrated from Poland and Russia. My father's ancestors are from Ireland. My mother was raised with Jewish traditions but disconnected herself from them long before I came into the world. My father grew up in a non-religious home but he attended Protestant churches since his youth.

As a result of my father's Christian leanings, I was brought up in a more Protestant home with only a nominal Jewish influence from my mother's side of the family. Therefore, the traditional Jewish Sabbath day of Friday evening and Saturday was just like any other day for my family. Sunday, however, was more of a special day for us. On Sundays we went to church, went out to eat for lunch, and then came home and did whatever we wanted for the rest of the day. Although I grew up in a Protestant-Christian environment, I started to feel the need to explore my Jewish roots during my adult years as I wanted to know more about the Jewish way of life.

My initial encounter with the Jewish community and culture was when I first visited Israel in 1995, during my senior year in college. I went there to spend three and a half months in a study abroad program in Jerusalem and to explore the biblical land where so much of history is centered. The time I spent in Israel literally changed my life in many ways, one of them being the practice of the Sabbath.

My first weekend in Jerusalem was unforgettable. It was the middle of a Friday afternoon and I noticed that all of the stores were closing one by one. When I asked someone to explain to me what was going on, they informed me that everyone was preparing for the Sabbath. "This must be some special day here in Israel," I thought to myself. That was the understatement of my college days. By sunset Friday evening, the city had become a ghost town. The buses had stopped running and there were almost no cars on the road. There weren't even any people walking around except for the more devout

Jews who were walking to and from their local synagogue, or to the Kotel (the Western Wall), the closest place a Jew can get to the location of the former Temple.

Week after week, I saw and experienced this same thing. From Friday evening until Saturday evening, there was nothing but calm and quiet. Since nothing significant was open during that time, I decided to enjoy this day of rest as well and it was like finding an old buried treasure! My weeks took on a whole different meaning after that. No longer was I looking at everyday the same anymore. I now saw that God intentionally gave us a pattern by which to live; work six days and take one day to rest as He did.

Thinking back on the last 15 years, I reflect on how I have struggled to protect my weekly Sabbath. Our world has become increasingly busy in all aspects, and in the multiculturalism of the United States I have found it even more challenging as there is no longer a cultural day of rest. Though many Americans still believe that practicing a weekly day of rest is a necessity, most people say it is nearly impossible to do so. This is true whether married, single, or part of a family.

There have been many books written about the Sabbath that tend to swing to one extreme or the other. These books either explain how to fulfill the Law in keeping the Sabbath or they spiritualize the Sabbath thus negating the need for physical rest. The focus of this book, therefore, will not be on either of these two extremes. It will, however, focus on assisting the reader within his community in practicing a weekly day of rest based on Jewish teachings and traditions, combined with connections to the New Testament.

Daniel Goldstein

Chapter 1

The Desire for the Sabbath: An Inner Longing

At night my soul longs for Thee,
Indeed, my spirit within me seeks
Thee diligently...
Isaiah 26:9a

It was a beautiful winter night with snow outside and I was enjoying an evening meal with a few friends around the dinner table. While we were eating, we were discussing the practice of a weekly day of rest. There is a beauty in living out this thing called "The Sabbath," which traditional Jewish people have been celebrating for thousands of years. For many around the table it was the first time this subject had ever been broached. For Bruce, however, it was something that he had thought long and hard about for years. However, he had been unable to fully integrate this practice into his life.

At one point during our discussion Bruce turned to me and said:

> *You know, Dan, I really agree with you regarding this idea about practicing a weekly Sabbath day of rest, and I've read a few books on this subject as well, but for whatever reason I've never been able to make it something that my family and I regularly practice. The books I have read explain the Sabbath but fall short of explaining how to make the Sabbath experience a reality. I've never been able to find anything to help me organize my day of rest with my wife and children.*
>
> *Most books about the Sabbath are written for individuals and focus on resting alone. These books also tend to spiritualize the Sabbath rather than providing helpful ideas about spending time together as a family.*

Bruce's words penetrated my soul.

Since coming back to my Jewish roots in my adult years and learning to practice the Sabbath as a way of life, I have been longing to write a book about the Sabbath to help many of my non-Jewish friends to see the beauty of this day of rest. However, since there have been so many books written about the Sabbath I was at a loss as to what the focus of my book should be. While Bruce was explaining his desire to practice the Sabbath with his family and his struggle to make it a reality, I understood what I wanted to write. I felt as though I had been one of the Israelites standing at the shore of the Red Sea with Pharaoh's troops in pursuit. I had felt stuck between a sea and an army and all of a sudden God opened the sea and I had somewhere to go.

When I understood Bruce's dilemma, a paradigm shift occurred in my mind. People do not want another book simply explaining the beauty of the Sabbath to them. The theology of the Sabbath and the importance of rest is a given for many of us. What is needed is a simple guide through this 24-hour period of time and space. So the heart cry of Bruce helped to bring clarity to my idea for a book. Therefore, I will attempt to write a practical book about the Sabbath day within a community of faith.

I truly believe that there are many people just like Bruce who desire to live out a day of rest once a week with their family but do not know where to begin. The soul indeed longs for God! One of the ways the soul meets with God is through rest. God gave us the Sabbath, and when we experience Sabbath rest we experience part of the essence of God. This book is devoted to helping us make this connection with God through the Sabbath.

Practicing a weekly Sabbath day of rest as a single person or simply by oneself is not overly difficult. It is easy to get in the car and go to the beach and simply spend the day watching the waves. We may go to the mountains, the desert, or to the park and read a book. The options for an individual are varied and easier to implement than for a family. When children of various ages are involved, it is much more challenging to properly plan how to spend a day together resting, eating, and playing. It is difficult because it takes a great deal of preparation. Society today in most parts of the world is not accustomed to this practice, so most people do not know where to begin.

In talking with different people about the Sabbath over the course of the past few years, I have found that most people know that the principle of practicing a weekly day of rest is necessary and good for their family and themselves. However, many have also convinced themselves that a weekly day of rest is nearly impossible considering all of the activities in which their family is involved. Perhaps this is the case for you and your family. Perhaps you believe that a weekly Sabbath day would be beneficial but somehow you cannot seem to make it a routine. This book has been especially written for you and for all of those who may benefit from a simple guidebook to help in planning a weekly day of rest.

My goal in writing this book is to enable others to enjoy a weekly Sabbath day that is spiritual, restful, and fun for the whole community, whether in a family setting or with a group of friends. To help the reader reach this goal this book includes explanations of Jewish traditions, ways to practically apply these traditions, and examples of how these traditions are connected to the New Testament. Beginning with Chapter 4, most chapters are divided into these three categories: **Jewish Tradition, Practical Applications, and New Testament Connections.**

The Basis of the Sabbath: Jewish Tradition

Since the Sabbath has been handed down through the years by the Jewish people, I have chosen to base the structure of this book on the way in which religious Jews traditionally practice the Sabbath. The religious, Jewish practice of the Sabbath is the most comprehensive outworking of this ancient tradition and God-given gift.

I am Jewish but I would not label myself as a "religious Jew." Rather, I am a Jew who is seeking to follow in the traditions of my ancestors. I, therefore, consider myself a "traditional Jew." While living among religious Jews, I have discovered the outworking of their lifestyle and will endeavor to portray this in an accurate way.

In this book I will refer often to "religious Jews." Understandably, there are a wide variety of "religious Jews." However, for the sake of clarity when I use the term "religious Jew" in this book I am referring to an orthodox Jew. An orthodox Jew is one who believes strongly in God, eats only kosher food, strives to keep the Law of God, and holds firmly to keeping the Sabbath. A religious Jewish man prays three times a day, wears a "*kippa*" (*yarmulke*) on his head, and also wears a four-cornered garment with tassels to remind him of the commands of God as defined in the Torah. While a religious Jew believes strongly in God and in the Law, it is important to note that his source of authority is found in the rabbis and in Jewish tradition.

I will also be referring to "traditional Jews." A traditional Jew is one who holds more loosely to a weekly Sabbath practice and generally eats only kosher foods. A traditional Jewish man may also wear a *kippa* on his head on the Sabbath or whenever he enters the synagogue.

Finally, I will also be referring to "secular Jews." A secular Jew typically does not believe in God. He may or may not eat kosher food and the Sabbath has no real significance in his or her life. A secular Jew almost never wears a *kippa* or enters a synagogue. The exception to this would be when attending a significant life event like a wedding or a *Bar Mitzvah*, or possibly once a year on *Yom Kippur*, The Day of Atonement.

While reading this book, keep in mind the differences between religious, traditional, and secular Jews. I will be drawing from the practices of both the religious and traditional Jews to explain the Sabbath.

There is no one way to describe the Sabbath practice because each Jewish family has their own unique traditions. Depending upon where the family roots originate (i.e. Morocco, Poland, Russia, Argentina, Iraq, etc...) the differences may be significant. Nevertheless, there are certain key elements that are standard during the Sabbath in most Jewish homes. I will share these in the pages that follow. I must state emphatically that the guidelines and structure that I provide in this book regarding the Jewish traditions and practices are not meant to be portrayed as a standard that others must observe. Rather, they are to be taken as they are, as valuable traditions that Christians and others can learn from and adapt to their unique family situations, with regard to practicing a Sabbath day of rest.

This book takes the reader through a traditional, Jewish Sabbath day. On the pages that follow one discovers how religious Jews prepare for the Sabbath, how they spend their time on the Sabbath, and how they uniquely commence and conclude the Sabbath. We will begin with the traditional candle lighting on Friday evening just before the Sabbath begins, to the closing Scriptures read in the synagogue as the Sabbath comes to an end on Saturday evening. Many of the details of the songs that are sung, the prayers that are prayed, and the blessings that are given throughout the Sabbath are included as well.

Utilizing Jewish Tradition to Create a Day of Rest

The Jewish blessings, songs, and prayers found in this book have been translated from Hebrew to English as much as possible to make this book "user friendly" and easy to understand.

Perhaps the Jewish prayers and blessings included in this book may be unfamiliar. I recommend that the reader accept the Jewish prayers and blessings as they are. It may be helpful to appreciate a culture that is different from one's own culture without feeling obligated to imitate the traditions presented.

This book is not meant to be a black and white, rigid type of instructional book regarding the Sabbath. Rather, as stated in the subtitle, it is "a guidebook" to practicing a weekly day of rest based on Jewish tradition. Each family and community endeavoring to establish a weekly day of rest within their situation will have distinct characteristics because of the uniqueness of their lives. This is the way it should be. Within very limited biblical guidelines there is no right or wrong way to practice a Sabbath day. There is a great deal of flexibility in practicing the Sabbath and I truly hope that what I have provided in this book will simply be a starting point and launching pad to creating a unique Sabbath experience for many.

Chapter 2

The Controversy of the Sabbath: "Is the Sabbath Still for Today?"

And on the Sabbath they rested
according to the commandment.
Luke 23:56b

I was born after the Bible had been all but dismissed from the public schools in the United States. During my high school years and throughout college, there were constant debates and government legislation centered on issues concerning "Judeo-Christian values." Questions concerning prayer in school, abortion, keeping "God" in or out of the Pledge of Allegiance, and related subjects of this nature were critical topics in the media.

A similar issue which relates to the above is whether or not to allow the Ten Commandments to remain in public buildings such as courthouses. Quite often the Association for the Civil Liberties Union (ACLU), or some other organization with a similar political agenda, challenges what had been previously believed to be traditional American values. These organizations declare that it is unconstitutional to have this religiously-based set of rules (the "Ten Commandments") engraved on public buildings or hung on the walls therein.

The interesting thing regarding this debate about the Ten Commandments is that the majority of the Judeo-Christian population in the US seems to strongly support the right for the Ten Commandments to be displayed in public buildings. This position is upheld on the grounds that the United States was founded on the premise that God does indeed exist, that we as human beings are created in His likeness, and that it is the role of the government to uphold these inalienable rights of its citizens to believe in Him. The moral basis of this position is the Bible, which combines the Jewish Holy Book as well as the Christian Holy Book.

If you and I truly believe that the Ten Commandments are a good set of rules by which to live, why is it that many within the Judeo-Christian society seem to pay so little attention to practicing the fourth commandment, *"Remember the Sabbath day, to keep it holy"*? The fourth commandment is the longest of the Ten Commandments and one that is repeated and spoken of throughout the Jewish Scriptures as well as the Gospels of the New Testament. One of the reasons for the repetition of the fourth commandment throughout the Scriptures seems to be because it is the one commandment that is broken most often by the Jewish people. Today, the majority of Jews still do not give much consideration to the Sabbath, though there are those who are called the "Religious" both in Israel and abroad that do try to keep the Sabbath as best they know how. On the Christian side there is considerable misunderstanding about how to practice a Sabbath day of rest incorporating New Testament teaching.

The Biblical Foundation of the Sabbath

Among those who accept the first five books of the Bible (the Torah) as God's Word, the Sabbath has its foundation in the account of the creation. It is actually the conclusion of an incredible week in which God finished everything He had planned to do! After God finished His work, these words were recorded in the book of Genesis:

> *And by the seventh day God completed His work which He had done; and He rested on the seventh day from all His work which He had done.*
> *Then God blessed the seventh day and sanctified it, because in it He rested from all His work which God had created and made.* (Genesis 2:2-3)

It is important to note that God set up a pattern in which to follow before the fall of man, before sin entered the world, pre-Moses, pre-Law, and before the Ten Commandments were ever given. God's pattern is to work six days and to rest one. Interestingly enough, most places around the world have a seven-day week whether they believe in God or not.

The Jewish Perspective of the Sabbath

God demonstrated the "work six days and rest one" pattern and then He officially implemented it into one of the Ten Commandments given to Moses (Exodus 20). The commandment of the Sabbath has been one of the defining characteristics of the Jewish people (Exodus 31:12-18). The Sabbath is the highlight of the week for the religious Jew, wherever he or she may live in the world. It is even referred to as "The Queen" in extra-biblical, Jewish writings with God having the place of the King. The Torah, God's Word, in any given synagogue is ornamented as a King having a crown resting on its top and clothed in a royal type of cloth. There is a sense of reverence due to approaching royalty as one draws near to God and His Word. This sense of reverence in the presence of royalty is also extended to the Sabbath as the "Queen of Days."

For the religious Jew, all week centers around preparing for this "holy day" which God has ordained from the beginning. The Jews have spent the last few thousand years fleshing out what it means to practice the Sabbath. One of the central focuses of the Sabbath is the absence of work. Throughout the centuries the rabbis have created a long list of positive and negative rules pertaining to the Sabbath as they have conceptualized what it means to work.

The Christian Perspective of the Sabbath

Many Christians believe that since Jesus was raised from the dead on the first day of the week, the Sabbath was therefore moved from the seventh day to the first. As a result, there are some Christians that keep a weekly day of rest on Sunday. There are other Christians who think that the Sabbath is a good idea; however, practicing it is not a reality for them. They may go to church on Sunday but then they go to work right after church finishes. There are also those in the Christian Church who say that the Sabbath is no longer valid or relevant. This particular theology is based on a teaching in the Church which says that the Sabbath is the only commandment of the "Ten" that is not repeated in the New Testament.

What does the New Testament really say about the Sabbath? Did Jesus come to bring an end to the Sabbath by the work He did on earth?

In the New Testament Jesus seems to constantly be getting Himself into trouble on the Sabbath. The religious leaders of His day gave Him a hard time for healing people on this special day. According to their understanding, He was breaking the law of the Sabbath by performing the work of healing.

On one occasion the religious leaders questioned Jesus with regard to why His disciples were not keeping the Sabbath. They were picking grain in the field and eating it. Jesus responds, *"But if you had known what this means, 'I DESIRE COMPASSION, AND NOT A SACRIFICE' you would not have condemned the innocent" (Matthew 12:7)*. Later, in this same text, Jesus was in the synagogue and there was a man there who had a shriveled hand. His accusers asked Him whether or not it was lawful to heal on the Sabbath. Jesus' response is in the form of a question:

> *What man shall there be among you, who shall have one sheep, and if it falls into a pit on the Sabbath, will he not take hold of it, and lift it out? Of how much more value then is a man than a sheep! So then, it is lawful to do good on the Sabbath. (12:11-12)*

And then He healed the man.

On another occasion while Jesus was teaching in a synagogue, He noticed a woman there who had a spiritual sickness that had left her bent over for eighteen years. Jesus took compassion on her and healed her. The response is then recorded in the Gospel of Luke:

> *And the synagogue official, indignant because Jesus had healed on the Sabbath, began saying to the multitude in response, 'There are six days in which work should be done; therefore come during them and get healed, and not on the Sabbath day.' But the Lord answered him and said, 'You hypocrites, does not each of you on the Sabbath untie his*

ox or his donkey from the stall, and lead him away to water him? And this woman, a daughter of Abraham as she is, whom Satan bound for eighteen long years, should she not have been released from this bond on the Sabbath day? And as He said this, all His opponents were being humiliated; and the entire multitude was rejoicing over all the glorious things being done by Him. (13:14-17)

It seems to me that Jesus never revoked the Sabbath or said that it was lawful to work seven days a week. He did, however, give an entirely new understanding concerning the practice of the Sabbath. He made it clear that the rules that the religious leaders had made concerning the Sabbath had missed the intent of God's law, the heart of the law!

One day when Jesus was asked the question concerning what is the greatest commandment, Jesus answered this way:

The foremost is, 'HEAR, O ISRAEL! THE LORD OUR GOD IS ONE LORD; AND YOU SHALL LOVE THE LORD YOUR GOD WITH ALL YOUR HEART, AND WITH ALL YOUR SOUL, AND WITH ALL YOUR MIND, AND WITH ALL YOUR STRENGTH.' The second is this, 'YOU SHALL LOVE YOUR NEIGHBOR AS YOURSELF.' There is no other commandment greater than these. (Mark 12:29-31)

Jesus combines the central belief of Judaism, "the Shma," (as above, beginning with "Hear") with another Jewish law regarding the caring for one's neighbor. In so doing, He summarizes the Ten Commandments into one law with two parts: Love God and love your fellow human being. Somewhere along the way, it seems that the religious leaders focused so much on trying to love God that the commandment to love their neighbor became less important.

The heart of Jesus' message seems to be that the two must go hand in hand, loving God and loving other human beings. If I may take some liberty to interpret Jesus' words, I believe He was saying that it is not only permissible but desirable to do acts of kindness on the Sabbath. It is desirable to help others on the Sabbath. It is even desirable to do things that may be considered work for the sake of saving a life. There is, in fact, a loophole even in the most religious circles of Jewish people today, translated as "saving a life" and this takes precedence over all. Just imagine if God Himself decided not to hear our prayers to heal or provide for us on the Sabbath or on the "Christian Holy Day," Sunday. We ought to be grateful that He is still merciful and does acts of kindness on our days of rest. Kindness, mercy, and performing acts of kindness to others do not cease because of the Sabbath. Likewise, the Sabbath does not cease to be what it is as a result of kindness to others. The Sabbath is a day of rest and freedom and must not be simply a religious rule to be followed.

Conclusion

My personal conclusion is that the Sabbath principle is still true for all humankind today; we are to work six days and enjoy one day to rest. On the Sabbath we are to leave our normal work routine and take pleasure in the relationships God has given us. This is true for the Jew as well as for the Christian. The Sabbath is something for human beings to benefit from and not meant to be a burden to endure. This is true despite ethnicity or religious heritage. With this understanding, let us consider how we may wisely choose a Sabbath day of rest.

Chapter 3

The Day of the Sabbath: Making a Wise Choice

The Sabbath was made for man,
and not man for the Sabbath.
Jesus (Mark 2:27)

Religious Jews keep a Sabbath day of rest on the seventh day, since this is the teaching in the Torah as well as the tradition. For Christians, however, there may be flexibility in choosing a day that is most appropriate for them.

There are those who teach that Gentile Christians must keep the law of the Sabbath in the same way as the Jewish people do. They believe that since they are governed by the same laws of the Torah, they too must keep the seventh day as a Sabbath. Christians that hold to this teaching are adhering to a principle commonly taught in the "One Law Movement." In the "One Law Movement" Christians are expected to live out their faith in a manner that is similar to religious Jews. They must adopt Jewish customs, and fulfill the Law through keeping all of the religious feasts. This includes the Sabbath. Daniel Juster & Russ Resnik (respected leaders within the Messianic Jewish Movement) respond to the teaching of the "One Law Movement" by saying,

...there is no word in the New Testament that exhorts Gentiles to circumcision, feasts, purity laws, Sabbaths, fast days and more, but that these practices were, and continue to be, central to Judaism. [1]

In agreement with Juster & Resnik, it is also my view that the Sabbath is a Jewish law that Gentile Christians are not legally obligated to keep. It is, however, a Jewish law with rich tradition and meaning that is embedded in the moral code of the Ten Commandments. Additionally, it offers a holistic way to practice a weekly day of rest. Therefore, I believe that Christians should not view the Sabbath as simply a law to keep, but rather embrace the command and moral fabric of the Sabbath just as they would the other nine commandments.

The Ten Commandments must be handled with great care and neither carried out in a legalistic way nor minimized to the point of irrelevance in our lives. In general, Christians today do not live out the Ten Commandments with all of the judicial punishments spoken of in the Old Testament. For example, Christians hold to the commandment that adultery is wrong and an abomination before Almighty God. However, they do not practice the instruction given in Numbers 5:11-31 which details how a husband is to deal with his wife if he even suspects her of having committed adultery. Let us explore in more detail what has brought about this radical shift in how the Old Testament commandments are to be observed by Christians.

While Jesus was on earth He taught His followers how to live out the teaching from the Torah as well as giving deep insight into the Ten Commandments. In one of Jesus' famous talks around the Sea of Galilee, Jesus stated:

Do not think that I came to abolish the Law or the Prophets; I did not come to abolish, but to fulfill. For truly I say to you, until heaven and earth pass away, not the smallest letter or stroke shall pass away from the Law, until all is accomplished. (Matthew 5:17-18)

Jesus communicates very clearly that He did not come to do away with the Law but to fulfill it, and warns those who are listening of the significance and eternal nature of the Law. There was much that was fulfilled in the Law by the life, death, and resurrection of Jesus. This is especially true with regard to the ceremonial and sacrificial laws. The moral Law, however, is carried over with some significant adjustments. One must understand how to practically live out the law as well as the punishments incurred for not doing so.

For example, continuing in the Gospel of Matthew, Jesus taught on the commandment regarding adultery:

You have heard that it was said, "YOU SHALL NOT COMMIT ADULTERY"; but I say to you, that everyone who looks on a woman to lust for her has committed adultery with her already in his heart. (Matthew 5:27-28)

Jesus takes the commandment about adultery to an even deeper level and includes the thoughts that one thinks. He makes this commandment something that anyone can apply to his or her life as a standard and not just a means to condemn a woman who has been caught in this act. Jesus makes a very similar statement with regard to murder being equated with anger towards one's brother. This, too, appears in this same chapter of Matthew (5:21-22). The Ten Commandments, therefore, are still valid for the followers of Jesus, but how they are lived out has an even deeper dimension. How can we apply Jesus' model of interpreting the commandments to the Sabbath?

In the book of Romans, Paul mentions the importance of each man being convinced in his own mind with regard to observing certain days (14:5). Additionally, in the letter to the Colossians there is a verse that instructs the followers of Jesus not to let others judge them regarding what they believe about the Jewish teachings of eating and drinking, celebrating the different religious holidays, recognizing the new moon, and Sabbath days (Colossians 2:16). It mentions these Jewish practices because Christianity has Jewish roots as Jesus Himself was Jewish and followed in the ways of Judaism. The majority of the early followers of Jesus were also Jewish. It was not until later that the followers of Jesus grew to include Gentiles as well.

In early Christianity there were various teachings concerning what the Gentile Christians did and did not have to practice with regard to the Jewish law and traditions. The verse in the letter to the Colossians mentioned above does not give many specific examples regarding these practices. It simply states not to let someone be judged by another with regard to them. Some Christians, unfortunately, may read this verse from Colossians and take it as an opportunity to disregard the Sabbath, thus living a life of constant activity, whether in a secular job or in "the ministry," seven days a week. I believe a person who thinks like this is greatly misled.

The context of this verse in Colossians is that believers in Jesus are to remember that their foundation is in Him as the Messiah and Lord and is not dependent upon their following rules and regulations (2:6-8). Jesus did not come to do away with the Law and the Prophets (the Hebrew Bible or Christian Old Testament) but to fulfill them (Matthew 5:17). By believing in Jesus as the fulfillment of the Law and the Prophets, there is a new basis of relationship with God (Colossians 2:1-3). A radical paradigm shift must take place in the life of one who believes in Jesus, i.e. recognizing that Jesus is the center of all wisdom and knowledge and that everything else is understood in the light of who He is!

There is, therefore, freedom before God as to how a believer in Jesus practices the Sabbath. Christians are not obligated to practice the Sabbath in the same way as the Jewish people are instructed to in the Torah. Jesus gives a more personal and deeper dimension to the meaning and intent of the Sabbath, together with the other nine commandments, through both His teaching and His lifestyle. The teaching in Colossians Chapter Two gives believers in Jesus total freedom to live out a Sabbath day as seems appropriate to them before Almighty God. I believe this also includes choosing a day of the week in which to rest.

How does one go about choosing a weekly day of rest?

The society in which people live, as well as their personal work schedule, may dictate their free day of the week. In the United States, a person may choose Saturday or Sunday as a day of rest as these days are typically non-work days and children are home from school. However, with our ever-increasing 24/7 (twenty four hours a day, seven days a week) working world, a person really might choose any day of the week and it may possibly even change from time to time.

When I lived in my father's house, as an adult, I would try to make Sundays my day of rest in compliance with his traditions. This usually fit best into my schedule as I worked a normal Monday through Friday job, ran errands on Saturday, and then rested on Sunday. This also worked well in the United States since Sundays have historically been the day of rest due to America's Christian heritage.

During another season in my life I was living in Istanbul, Turkey, and I had a very different schedule there. Turkey has a unique culture in that it is a largely Muslim nation with a democratic government. It has adopted a western style of a Monday through Friday or Saturday work week with Sunday being a typical day of rest. There is no official "day of rest" in Turkey, as in Judaism and Christianity, and some Turks even work seven days a week. As an English teacher in Istanbul, the demands were put upon me to work both Saturdays and Sundays because this is when most people have free time and want to use it to learn English.

My schedule evolved over time in Istanbul and looked very different from anything I had experienced before. It took deliberate effort and practice to hone it into something practical and culturally relevant. In so doing it didn't take too long for me to rule out Saturday or Sunday as a day of rest. Between my work schedule on the weekends and private lessons during the week, I realized I had to pick a certain day and keep it as my Sabbath day so that I might rest and enjoy life rather than work. During that time in my life, Mondays wound up being an optimal choice for my day of rest and, believe it or not, God met with me on Mondays and gave me rest.

What is the best day for you?

In order for you and your family or community to ensure success in designating a weekly Sabbath day you must be aware of certain pitfalls. You need to consider the society in which you live, your work schedule, your family, and any other responsibilities you may have in your life. You may not have the flexibility to choose a weekday as I did in Istanbul and you may have to do the best you can with a Saturday or Sunday. No day will be completely perfect.

Avoiding the "Religious Activity" Traps

When I was growing up, my father took my sisters and me to church with him every Sunday. We would generally go to Sunday school followed by the main church service, which took up most of the morning. After lunch we would have a couple of hours to do whatever we wanted and then, at approximately 5pm, we would eat something and prepare for the evening church activities. I usually went to an evening youth meeting followed by another church service. This was our day of REST?

Some of you may not agree, but I do not subscribe to this type of schedule contributing to or comprising a day of rest. For me it became a day of church activity with a great deal of driving around in the family car. Interestingly enough I have discovered that it is not much different in the synagogue setting. In my adult years I find that I am spending increasing amounts of time attending the synagogue along with the different activities surrounding the Jewish lifestyle. I do not like to oversimplify and I am sure there are variations of this, but I will try to explain what I have seen and experienced in the Jewish world.

The Jewish Sabbath begins on Friday evening and continues until Saturday evening with a considerable amount of that time spent going back and forth to the synagogue. The synagogue is generally within walking distance from one's home, so there is no transportation stress. On Friday evening the men (and possibly women and children) will make their way to the synagogue for Kabbalat Shabbat, the welcoming of the Sabbath. This is a shorter service that lasts approximately an hour. The Kabbalat Shabbat service takes place as the sun is setting. At the end of the service people return to their homes to enjoy the special Sabbath meal together.

The main service in the synagogue is held on Saturday morning and this gathering lasts between two and three hours. There are also social times after the Friday evening and Saturday morning services with food and drinks at the synagogue (depending on the synagogue and local culture). On Saturday evening the concluding meetings take place: the evening prayers followed by "*Havdalah*." *Havdalah* is a ceremony which marks the conclusion of the Sabbath and emphasizes the separation between the holy (the Sabbath) and the secular (the six-day work week). In the United States, where Sunday is also a typical day off from work and school, synagogues usually host Sunday school, which may include Hebrew lessons or some sort of religious class.

Religion most assuredly has a way of helping us fill our free time, for better or for worse! Whether one is a Jew or a Christian, the day of rest seems to be easily swallowed up in activity. Please consider that I have not even mentioned how "committee meetings" can easily sneak into these days of 'rest' due to the convenience of everyone already being together.

One may ask why I point out the practice of the Jewish Sabbath as being overly busy, since the basis of this book is practicing a day of rest in community based on traditional Judaism. I mention this to simply illustrate that business can enter into any Sabbath day of rest. That being said, there are some major differences in how I have seen the Jews live out their Sabbath day compared to those in the Christian world. First of all, as I mentioned, the synagogue is almost always located within walking distance from one's home, therefore, the stress of driving is alleviated. Secondly, the family spends most of the time together during the Sabbath, with a major emphasis on meal times that are filled with conversation and are meant to be relaxing and rejuvenating. Thirdly, the Sabbath for religious Jews will always be at least twenty four hours. This is a full day compared to just the day of Sunday for some Christians (possibly twelve hours). There is much to be learned from the traditional practice of the Jewish Sabbath.

In conclusion, we ought to think about and decide upon the following questions: When is the best day to truly enjoy a day of rest? Which activities are necessary to participate in on the day of rest?

When choosing a day of rest we must take into account all the meetings and activities that are scheduled daily, and seek to find the best time to truly escape the normal business of the week. The day one worships within a local community may or may not be the best day to practice the Sabbath. Choose a Sabbath day as a family or community and decide upon activities in which to participate. This will ensure a restful experience and not just another busy day.

Chapter 4

The Context of the Sabbath: Community

Two are better than one
because they have
a good return for their labor.
Ecclesiastes 4:9

The Bible gives very few details with regard to how one should keep the Sabbath. The main idea seems to be that neither the individual nor those abiding in his home should do any work at all. However, there is almost nothing in the biblical text about what one SHOULD DO on the Sabbath. As a result of this, historical teachings of the rabbis combined with traditions that have been handed down since the days of Moses, have helped to form what we now know as the Jewish practice of the Sabbath. One of the core elements herein has been the family unit. Celebrating the Sabbath with one's family provides the natural community in which to carry out this holy day.

Jewish Tradition

In the traditional Jewish home there are very clear distinctions as to the roles each one has leading up to and during the Sabbath. Women are the keepers of the home and therefore they are the ones that are generally responsible for the meals, especially the Erev Shabbat meal on Friday evening. The men (including the boys) are generally the students of the Torah, Mishnah, Talmud and other religious books. They guide the Sabbath meal along with the prayers and discussions surrounding the particular Scripture that is read. The Sabbath begins when the woman of the house lights the candles and extends until the last blessing or song is sung into the late hours of Friday evening and continues throughout the day on Saturday. The children are also involved in different aspects of the Friday night meal and throughout the Sabbath, depending on their age and ability to participate.

The Sabbath, for children of religious families, is met with great expectation. The children wear their best clothes, and both boys and girls study the Torah ahead of time so as to be prepared and to be able to contribute something of spiritual significance. Most notably however, the children simply enjoy spending time with the family, having focused attention from mom and dad, and playing games with different members of the family.

The family unit is given great value in Judaism, and observing the Sabbath creates a forum in which family time occurs in a natural and positive way.

The Natural Community - Family

During my time in Israel it has been fascinating to meet many people who are married adults with children who make it a point to spend the Sabbath with their parents. They may travel an hour or two weekly or every other week in order to achieve this. The Israeli military encourages this practice as well. Since service in the Israeli military is compulsory, the enlisted men and women generally serve Sunday through Thursday and then return home for the weekend. This generally occurs every other weekend so that time may be spent on the Sabbath (Friday night and Saturday) with families. Additionally, soldiers are even given extra time on Sunday morning to get back to their bases so as not to take away from the post-Sabbath celebrations Saturday evening.

There is a saying in the United States that says something like "The family that prays together stays together." When I think about the Sabbath celebration amongst the Jewish people I think it could be said, "The family that celebrates the Sabbath together stays together." This is not to undermine the value of prayer. In fact, the reader will come to see that prayer is an integral part of the Sabbath celebration.

The topic at hand is recognizing the value of certain practices that will enable the family to unite in such a way as to make it a stronger force or a community with purpose that will change the world. The practice of the Sabbath goes so far beyond a barbecue on the Fourth of July (United States Independence Day), a Thanksgiving meal, a week of celebrating Christmas or Hanukkah, or even a holiday vacation in Hawaii. These are good things for families to do together, to build memories, to remember their faith, and simply to have "family time." However, these events may be quite distant from each other in relation to time. If one misses a Thanksgiving meal or a vacation with the family one year, it may be another year before one has the chance to participate again. The practice of the Sabbath is weekly and therefore habitual. It is this frequency and regularity of celebration which provide a stable and concrete environment in which to build unity and instill values within a trusted community.

What if you do not belong to a family?

There are many people who, for one reason or another, find themselves without a family. Someone may be single, widowed, divorced, away at college or in the military, or any one of countless other situations. The natural family environment in which to practice and celebrate the Sabbath in community is missing. I am well acquainted with this situation as I am single, have never been married, and have lived in different places in the United States and around the world.

There are many different ways to handle those situations when one does not have a natural community. In Jewish society one can more easily find a solution to this problem through a local synagogue or a Jewish agency. There are many Jewish families willing and able to host those who are newcomers or alone in order to celebrate the Sabbath. This is especially true for the evening meal on Friday. Christian communities may or may not have this venue with which to absorb single people into their families. It depends upon the local culture and a variety of other factors. If this is not a common practice in your community, you will need to be creative.

Since I am Jewish, I have had the opportunity to become part of different Jewish communities to celebrate the Sabbath. However, I have also had times in my life when I simply did not have a Jewish community around me. At those times I have had to compensate for this. I have learned over the years to find people who are interested in this ancient tradition and to ask them if they would like to start practicing it together, whatever their ethnicity may be.

Some Jews may disagree with me on this point (celebrating the Sabbath with non-Jews) but it seems clear to me from the Torah that when God blessed our father Abraham, He told him that all nations of the earth would be blessed through him

(Genesis 22:18). It was to Abraham's descendants that God would fulfill this blessing as He brought the Israelites into existence and gave them His Torah and His Holy Scriptures so that they may be exemplified within community and be a light to the nations (Isaiah 49:6; 60:1-3). From the book of Isaiah we can also learn that God gave very clear instructions regarding Gentiles who wanted to walk in God's ways. God specifically says, "For My house will be called a house of prayer for ***all the peoples***" (Isaiah 56:7). Based on these Scripture references, it seems clear that God would be pleased for Jews to sharc their heritage with those around them as they live out His ways and purposes before the nations.

Practical Applications:
Make Your Own Community

Adopt a family

If you find yourself alone and without a family in which to develop community, I suggest that you approach someone you already know who has a family and ask them if they would be interested in having a weekly Sabbath celebration together. Through the weekly practice of getting together, sharing a meal (or meals), and talking about life you will build strong community with one another.

During my time in Istanbul I asked an American friend of mine with whom I worked if he and his wife together with their children would be interested in celebrating the Sabbath. They agreed, and from time to time we would have a Sabbath type meal together with some of the traditional practices. Although they have eight children, they always had room at their table for another person and enjoyed learning about and practicing the Sabbath with me. I should mention that I did not usually spend the night at their home and so we did not spend a full day together. We simply enjoyed one evening a week together over a meal, Sabbath style. It was a beginning, and gave us a glimpse into what the Sabbath was intended to be.

Create a Family Environment with Friends

Another option is to create your own family environment with a group of friends. Present this concept of the Sabbath to your friends and discuss the possibilities of making it work together in community. One person could host the Sabbath in their home each week or you could have a rotating schedule of a few different homes; in that way, all the preparations of hosting would not devolve upon the same person each week.

I have practiced the Sabbath with this type of community as well. Sometimes it was a group of men, sometimes it was a mixed group of men and women, or even a married couple and some singles. The point was not to have an "ideal family" type of get-together. Rather, it was to have a workable community with which to meet over a relaxed meal, to talk about our lives, discuss God's Word, and build some memories.

One way we did this was to have an evening meal once a week. I would make the main course and friends who came each brought something to contribute. Another way we created community was that we would gather after the Sunday morning worship time. My friends and I stopped by the grocery store, bought what we needed for a meal, and then made our way to one of our homes. We prepared a big afternoon meal together and then enjoyed it. We played the guitar and sang some songs. We talked about God's Word and prayed for one another. Our time together lasted seven or eight hours from 10 am until 5 or 6 pm and it was a refreshing sense of community. Creating community with friends around a Sabbath day of rest is life-changing!

Host an Open House with Housemates

If you are single and live with other people, you have the opportunity to create community in your own home. It can be a community based on those who live in the house or you could invite other friends to join you as well. All of those living in the home need to agree upon how your Sabbath will be organized, how responsibilities will be divided, and who will be invited. Since it should be a semi-formal type of meal, you will need to know approximately how many guests will be included week to week or it may become unmanageable. Plan well and enjoy a Sabbath with a group of friends in your home.

In Israel I have encountered a unique and creative community similar to the one I have just described. There were some young ladies I got to know who were all single and shared a home together in Jerusalem. There were usually about five or six women living in their house at any given time. Since they had no family close by, they often hosted a Sabbath meal on Friday evenings and invited friends (male and female) to join them. They would clean and organize their home on Friday, worked together to prepare the meal, and then guided the evening in such a way that it was enjoyable for everyone. The friends who were invited generally brought something to contribute to the meal as well: a salad, dessert, wine, and so forth. On any given Friday evening there would be anywhere from ten to twenty people in their home. It was great fun and created a unique sense of community.

Utilize the Community In Which You Are Involved

Another way of creating community is to incorporate the practice of the Sabbath with a group of people with whom you are already involved. It could be a sports team, people you exercise or work with, a musical band, a Bible study group, or some other unique community. If you consider the people in your life and the different network of friends that you have, you may find that you already have a group of people with whom to create Sabbath community.

I once had the opportunity to celebrate the Sabbath with friends (ten men) while we were away for a ski trip in the mountains. We stayed in a log cabin in the woods and had a great weekend together. I offered to organize a Sabbath meal for us on Saturday and everyone agreed. We had an amazing day of rest, enjoyed the meal together, and had wonderful conversations. It was a grand Sabbath and a beautiful memory with a special group of friends. A Sabbath community sprang up from this group of men that continues to this day.

I did not have to create this group of friends. We all knew each other and we were getting together weekly before we went away on this trip. I simply offered to organize a Sabbath type evening while we were away and everyone agreed. If you already have a community of friends who know each other, are in regular contact, and are open to practicing a weekly day of rest together, then this would be a logical place to commence your Sabbath practice.

Reality Check

For those who find themselves in this category of needing to create some type of community for the Sabbath, I encourage you to start small and let things grow and develop. In the beginning you may not be able to convince friends to commit to a full twenty four hours of Sabbath rest together. However, they may be interested in having the weekly evening meal together to welcome or begin the Sabbath, and then to have separate plans for the following day. As a single person it may be more challenging to develop the full twenty four hour Sabbath day in community, but the key is to start small and build from there.

Developing the weekly Sabbath experience will take perseverance, continual prayer, and patience as you work together with God to bring this about. I want to encourage you to persevere even when others do not want to get involved. The Sabbath can never be forced on anyone. It must be a desire from within that one chooses to explore. Begin with the time and people that God has given you at the moment and wait on Him as you take steps forward. As I have explained in the examples given above, I have created some beautiful Sabbath memories with different groups of friends in various settings. Be creative and flexible!

The Value of Community

Whatever your situation may be, there are dozens of ways to build community and create an atmosphere of enjoyment as you think about your day of rest. It must be noted, however, that it can easily become a day that you begin to dread if you end the day feeling overworked or discover that you are more of an introvert than you had previously realized. The community aspect of the Sabbath is only effective if it produces joy and a sense of peace. It must not add stress to your life. In fact, you may prefer not to have community as part of your Sabbath. If you find that you are able to rest and draw closer to God by practicing the Sabbath alone (without a community), then this may be the best option for you.

As much as I enjoy people, there are times when I simply prefer to be by myself and spend a day alone. At times such as these, it is God and me, and we usually find ourselves enjoying the beauty of nature. I have used friends' beach homes and mountain homes for this very purpose. I usually choose the "off season" and spend a couple of days alone to think, pray, and just separate myself from the world for a time. The Sabbath can be a time to do this, as well. Maybe you are a young adult living at home, working a full-time job, and you see your family daily. For you, a day alone at the beach may be exactly what is needed for rest and rejuvenation.

Community can be a valuable aspect of celebrating and practicing the Sabbath. However, God did not command us to be in community on the Sabbath nor need we be. Each person needs to evaluate his or her situation and decide how he or she will choose to spend one day a week in a special way and in a way that enables rest, restoration, and enables us to draw closer to God.

As a general principle, however, I do encourage community to be a part of your Sabbath in some way. This will help to provide the weekly accountability that we all need in our lives. The focus of this book is on practicing the Sabbath in community so there will not be much more said about practicing the Sabbath alone. Choose your community and let the Sabbath begin.

New Testament Connections

The Christian sense of community is reflected throughout the New Testament. Jesus modeled it with His disciples and it is something that has continued since He physically ascended to heaven. One account of this is found in the book of The Acts of the Apostles:

> *And they were continually devoting themselves to the apostles' teaching and to fellowship, to the breaking of bread and to prayer.* (Acts 2:42)

This verse is often a standard for Christians meeting together. Generally, time is spent eating, praying, and receiving teaching concerning spiritual things. The practice of the Sabbath is a perfect way to live this out.

Note: From this point on, since family is the traditional environment in which community exists, I will use the term "family" in this book, encompassing both the traditional family unit and community in all of its various forms. When emphasis is needed I will use both the words, family and community, to differentiate and clarify.

Community: Community generally consists of a variety of people from different backgrounds. Communities may include people from different age groups. Community may also include any variety of married couples, children, and single adults.

Chapter 5

The Commencement of the Sabbath: A Prelude to Rest

So we carried on the work... from dawn
until the stars appeared.
Nehemiah 4:21

One of the important aspects of observing a weekly Sabbath is being aware of an official time when it commences. Most people ordinarily think of a day beginning in the morning at the rising of the sun; the Jewish concept of a day, however, actually begins in the evening, at the setting of the sun. This understanding has been taken from the creation account in which God spent six days creating this complex universe in which we live. At the end of each day it is written, "It was evening and it was morning, one day" and so forth until the end of the week. This is where the Jewish understanding that a day begins in the evening originated. Hence, the Jewish practice of the Sabbath begins on the evening before the actual day of the Sabbath. It is important, therefore, to determine when an evening actually begins. How does one determine the exact beginning of an evening?

Jewish Tradition

A Specific Time

It is commonly accepted that an evening begins at the setting of the sun, however, this is not a precise time. To be safe, the rabbis have set the beginning of the Sabbath an hour before the setting of the sun so as to protect people from working right up to the start of the Sabbath. The important element here is to have some criteria which enable everyone to know that they have now crossed the line from the six days of the week to the seventh day. They have completed the days of work and have entered the day of rest. They have arrived at a time which is no longer ordinary but has been set apart as holy.

Most things in life have an official time in which they begin. If one is going to host a party one does not only tell people on which day the party will be held. The natural question in everyone's mind (at least for those in the West) is what time this party will begin. People want to know how to plan their day accordingly so that they can enjoy the party and not show up too early and waste their own time or too late and miss it. Everything has its beginning and so it is with the Sabbath.

The Candles

The Jewish Sabbath begins on Friday evening after the sun has gone down. Sabbath candles are generally lit by the woman of the home (although, they can be lit by a man if there is no woman in the home). The candles are always lit before the sun goes down so as not to do any work on the Sabbath. Lighting a fire is forbidden on the Sabbath, as is written in the Torah. As a general guideline the candles are lit at least eighteen minutes before the sun sets and the following blessing is read after lighting:

Blessed are you, O Lord our God, King of the universe,
Who has made us holy in His commandments
and commanded us to light the candles of the Sabbath.

As is the case with many of the blessings incorporated into the Sabbath tradition, they are not easily identified in the Torah or biblical text. Since the destruction of the second Temple nearly 2000 years ago, many commands and practices associated with the Temple are now incorporated into religious practices in the synagogue or practiced during the Sabbath at home. This seems to be the case with the practice of lighting the Sabbath candles, as well.

I have not found a teaching in the Torah directly related to lighting candles for the Sabbath. However, there is clear teaching about lighting the lamps of the Temple every evening to keep them continuously burning from evening to morning (Exodus 27:20-21). Therefore, in lighting the candles of the Sabbath one can have in mind that Almighty God commanded His people to have candles (an oil lamp) continually lit before Him in the Temple. Sabbath candles are lit just before the Sabbath and burn out at some point during the evening; therefore, the meaning here is more symbolic, as candles are not continually burning throughout the Sabbath day.

Everything about the Sabbath has meaning and so it is with the candles. Many rabbis teach that the two candles are symbolic reminders of what God commanded His people when He gave them the Ten Commandments; ***to remember the Sabbath and keep it holy*** as is stated in the fourth commandment. There are, therefore, a minimum of two candles that are lit just before the Sabbath, although people may light more. In some families, it is traditional for the young women who have arrived at Bat Mitzvah age (twelve years of age) to light candles as well.

There is another meaning that can be derived from the Sabbath candles, this being in connection to something known as *"shlom bayit,"* peace and contentment in the home. Candles are used for different occasions, but typically for special occasions, birthdays, weddings, romantic evenings, and things of this nature. Candles are used on the Sabbath because they add light to the occasion, mark it as significant, and add a bit of tranquility to the evening, separating it from the other six days of the week.

A Typical Sabbath Beginning

The traditional Friday evening commencement of the Sabbath begins with a lavish meal with a great deal of food. The purpose is not to gorge oneself but simply to have nothing lacking on this night. It is to be a meal that is enjoyed without having to prepare anything else. It is a meal that will satisfy all that sit at the table. Before the actual meal, though, there are many traditions that are integrated throughout the evening to help appreciate and savor this unique time.

By the time the sun has set the preparations for the Sabbath should be finished. There is generally no more cooking, cleaning, setting the table or even dressing oneself. These things are to be done before the evening begins. The candles are lit, the table is set, and the food has been prepared and is ready to be served. Since the Bible explicitly speaks of not making a fire on the Sabbath, religious Jews do not typically do any more cooking during this time. Be assured, however, that Jews in our modern age do not eat cold meals throughout the Sabbath. Most traditional Jewish homes today have electric food warmers that pots and casserole dishes can be placed upon to keep them warm. These warmers are turned on before the Sabbath begins, left on for the duration of the Sabbath, and food is placed on them hours beforehand.

When I was a newcomer to Israel I began attending a local synagogue and was frequently invited to the home of the rabbi of that synagogue. At home were his wife, their seven children, his mother, and his 100-year-old grandmother. Despite such a full home, he was still kind enough to invite me to join them. I have fond memories of my Sabbaths with them and my perspective of the Sabbath has been positively affected by my times in their home. Much of what I share here in this chapter will be based on occasions with them, combined with experiences at the homes of other friends along the way. What then does the flow of a typical Sabbath evening look like?

Sabbath Songs/Blessings at the Synagogue

Before the meal is eaten there are traditional blessings that are practiced to welcome the Sabbath. The Sabbath blessings actually begin in the synagogue where the Sabbath is ushered in. Generally, men attend the Friday night service in the synagogue; however, women and children are welcome to attend as well. If women and children are not in attendance, they are usually at home waiting for their husbands and fathers to return so they can begin the traditions at home.

During a classic Friday night service at the synagogue there is a focus on worshipping God and welcoming the Sabbath with special psalms, songs, and blessings. Psalm 29, 92-93, and 95-99 are typical psalms that are either read or sung. Psalm 92 is especially important because this particular psalm was written specifically for the Sabbath day. It is actually detailed in the superscript at the head of this Psalm in the English translation, *"A Psalm, a Song for the Sabbath day."* This is literally the first sentence in the Hebrew text emphasizing that this particular Psalm was written for the Sabbath. Because of this Psalm's focus on the Sabbath day it is traditional to recite it on this special day.

After a formal welcoming of the Sabbath at the synagogue, everyone makes their way home to continue the celebrations. As people leave the synagogue, everyone greets each other with the traditional Sabbath greeting, "*Shabbat Shalom*!" After everyone returns from the synagogue they take their places around the table. The table is adorned with flowers that have recently been cut or bought, chairs are added as needed, and everyone sits down and gets comfortable. There are many songs, prayers, and blessings that are part of the Sabbath tradition in the home as well. Some of these are part of every Sabbath while others are optional. When I say optional I mean that one can choose from a plethora of songs, blessings, and prayers that they would like to use. Some of these songs and prayers are psalms taken directly from the book of Psalms in the Bible, for example Psalm 23.

Sabbath Songs/Blessings in the Home

Following the short service at the synagogue, the family traditions come alive in the home after everyone has returned. One of the traditional songs that is sung on Friday evening in just about every Jewish home is "*Shalom Aleichem*" [translated: "Peace unto you (plural)"] which is a song welcoming the ministering angels during the Sabbath. It is a song/prayer to invite the angels, asking them to come in peace, bless those in the home with peace, and depart in peace. This song is supported by the portion of Scripture found in Psalm 91:9-15 with a focus on verse 11 which states, *"For He will give His angels charge concerning you, To guard you in all your ways."* The context of this verse focuses on the person who trusts in God and, as a result, experiences God's care and protection. When this song is sung the singers recall the promises of God. They remember that as they are doing what God has commanded them to do, they in return will receive God's protection around them through His angels.

It is worth noting here that religious Jews do not use instruments of any sort on the Sabbath. Therefore, all songs are sung without any musical accompaniment. There are many things that are forbidden for religious Jews on the Sabbath, playing an instrument being one of them. I am not of the same mind regarding this issue, especially since the key Psalm relating to the Sabbath, Psalm 92, states specifically in the text that it is written for the Sabbath and lists several instruments in verse three of this chapter. The instruments are used to make music while worshipping God on the Sabbath. For this reason I personally believe God takes pleasure in our making music to Him on the Sabbath with instruments.

Family Blessings

Another traditional Friday evening song/blessing is called "*Eshet Hayil*" in Hebrew and is traditionally translated into English as "an excellent wife" or "a virtuous woman" or even "a women of valor." It can also be translated from Hebrew as "a woman of force/strength" and we know by the context and surrounding verses that it refers to a woman who is a faithful wife and an excellent mother. This song is basically a blessing from a husband over his wife (and the mother of his children) taken directly from the Proverbs of Solomon, chapter 31, verses 10-31; it is an acrostic.

The book of Proverbs in the Bible is generally called the Proverbs of Solomon. However, Proverbs 31 is actually accredited to "...King Lemuel, the oracle which his mother taught him..." as the first verse of this chapter clearly states. My suspicion is that King Lemuel's mother was reminding him of the kind of woman he should choose for marriage.

This proverb is sung by the men at the table and is a reminder of the great value of the woman of the home. It is at this time that the wife and/or mother of the home is honored for all the little things that may have been overlooked during the week. By taking care of the affairs that concern the welfare of the family and the home, she shows her reverence and fear of God. In the singing of this song, the unmarried girls at the table are given a picture of the ideal Jewish wife and mother, and the young men are reminded of the kind of woman they are to wait for and marry. It is beautiful poetry with deep meaning and contains applicable principles for today even though it was written over 3000 years ago.

After the blessing of the wife is complete, the blessings over the children begin. There are specific blessings spoken over the children, and there are different blessings for sons and daughters. At this point in the evening I have typically seen the father (and sometimes the mother) of the home get out of his chair and place his hands on the heads of each of his children, one by one, as he prays a short blessing over them:

Blessing over a son:

May God make you like Ephraim and Manasseh!

Blessing over a daughter:

May God make you like Sarah, Rebecca, Rachel, and Leah.

General Blessing: (spoken over a son or daughter)

The LORD bless you and keep you;
The LORD make His face shine on you,
And be gracious toward you:
The LORD lift up His countenance on you,
And give you peace.

The blessing over a son is taken directly from Genesis 48:20. The blessing over a daughter is something that has been adapted through the ages and has its root in the blessing that

Rebecca received directly from her family in Genesis 24:60, combined with the blessing that is given to Boaz on behalf of his bride, Ruth. In the portion found in the book of Ruth, the elders of Bethlehem pronounced a blessing saying, "*May the LORD make the woman who is coming into your home like Rachel and Leah, both of whom built the house of Israel;*" (Ruth 4:11). These blessings are then followed by the Scripture found in Numbers 6:24-26 where God instructs Moses in the manner that the sons of Israel are to be blessed. This is also called the Aaronic blessing.

Kiddush, The Blessing over the Wine

After the blessing of the family members, the *kiddush* is recited. The *kiddush* is the blessing over the wine (or grape juice). The word "*kiddush*" is simply a Hebrew word which means sanctification. This is a solemn act that uses wine to sanctify and set apart this special day, the Sabbath. What is the reason that wine in particular is used to set this day apart from the others?

The use of wine as a sanctifying act is first recorded in the book of Genesis chapter 14. In this account Abraham (his name being "Abram" at this point) has just rescued his nephew Lot after he was taken captive. Immediately following this event it is recorded that a certain king goes out to meet Abraham. Here is the account from the text:

> *And Melchizedek king of Salem brought out bread and wine; now he was a priest of God Most High. And he blessed him and said, 'Blessed be Abram of God Most High, Possessor of heaven and earth;*
> *And blessed be God Most High,*
> *Who has delivered your foes into your hand.*
>
> (Genesis 14:18-19)

Why does King Melchizedek bring out the bread and wine? It seems that the bread and wine are indicators of something significant. One of the foundational meanings of the bread and wine together is for the purpose of sanctification or setting something or someone apart. In this account from Genesis 14, King Melchizedek was celebrating the victory Abraham had just won. I also believe that Melchizedek was setting Abraham apart as God's man on earth and he used the bread and wine to tangibly illustrate this as he spoke words of blessing over Abraham. The wine as illustrated here in Genesis 14 is something which is used to sanctify, and in this case the object of sanctification was a man, Abraham.

In another section of the Bible there is an opposite use of wine for the purpose of sanctification. The Nazirite vow is a pledge taken in order to separate oneself unto God for a time. In the giving of the Nazirite vow in Numbers 6, God instructs Moses regarding the rules for carrying out this practice. The first rule is to **abstain** from wine. From the time one takes the Nazirite vow until it ends, he or she is commanded not to drink wine or grape juice and not even to eat grapes or raisins. There is no specific reason given for this regulation; however, we are able to understand from this teaching that the partaking of and abstaining from the fruit of the vine in all of its forms have powerful connotations.

On the Sabbath, wine is used to sanctify this special day and set it apart from the other six days. Wine (typically red) is poured into a wine glass or a special Sabbath goblet with a small plate underneath it to catch any wine that may spill over. Before the actual blessing over the wine, the text from Genesis 1:31 - 2:3 is read or sung, reminding everyone present why this day is so special, following the pattern God established as He rested on the seventh day. Traditionally, everyone stands while this passage from the Bible is read.

After the reciting of the portion of Scripture from Genesis 1-2, the blessing over the wine is recited. The blessing over the wine in Hebrew is simply an acknowledgement that God is God, the King of the universe and that everything we have comes from Him. The blessing over the wine is filled with phrases reminding everyone at the table that we are setting apart this day from the other days and acknowledging that this is in accordance with God's commandment. In the beginning of this blessing there is a specific blessing regarding the wine. Here is the English translation of the blessing:

Blessed are you, O Lord our God, King of the universe, Creator of the fruit of the vine.

The man or father of the home stands and holds the Sabbath goblet in his hands while everyone else at the table stands with him. He then reads the section from Genesis 1-2 followed by the above blessing over a full cup of red wine that has a bit of water added to it. The rabbis teach that wine can symbolize judgment and water can symbolize mercy so a little mercy (water) is added to soften the judgment (wine). Immediately after he finishes reading the blessing over the wine, he continues to recite a short blessing regarding the sanctity of the Sabbath. The father then drinks and shares from his cup with the others at the table. They either drink straight from his cup or he pours wine from his cup into their cups, which already have some wine in them. Either way, after the blessing is completed all say "Amen" and drink in agreement with the blessing.

Since the cup of wine is full and it is usually overflowing, there is a little plate under the special Sabbath goblet (*kiddush* cup) to catch the overflow. After the cup is drunk the excess is poured into the goblet and drunk as well. This overflowing cup is a symbol of the fullness of joy and life that God gives us. We are grateful for all of His blessings in our life and remember that everything we have, including the fullness of life, comes from His hand alone. The excess wine is drunk, and not simply thrown away, because of the sanctity of the *kiddush* wine.

The Blessing over the Hands

After the blessing over the wine is completed and partaken of, religious Jews will practice the tradition of the washing of the hands. The hands are generally washed in a certain fashion, pouring water from a cup on each hand three times starting with the right hand. Afterward, a short blessing is said as the clean hands are elevated. Here is the English translation of the blessing:

Blessed are you, O Lord our God, King of the universe,
who has made us holy by His commandments
and commanded us concerning the washing of the hands.

There are many reasons for the hand washing ceremony and one of the primary purposes is to have clean hands before touching the bread. Bread is the other main substance from the earth that is used to sanctify the Sabbath meal. However, unlike the wine which is drunk from a glass, one must actually pick up the bread with his or her hands to eat it. Out of respect for the sanctity of the elements, hands are washed so as to treat the bread with respect for that which God has given to sustain life.

Worth noting here is the Hebrew word used for "washing." The word is transliterated "*netilat*" and can also be translated as the act of "lifting." Today both actions are commonly practiced amongst religious Jews, the washing and the lifting. The hands are washed, lifted to at least eye level, the blessing is stated, and then the hands are dried with a towel. More about this practice will be mentioned later in this chapter.

The Blessing over the Bread

The bread is covered with a special cloth before the evening starts to keep it set apart until it is blessed and eaten. The cloth covering for the bread usually has the words "*Shabbat Shalom*" embroidered on it. "*Shabbat Shalom*" is the greeting given to one another on the Sabbath. It simply means "the peace of the Sabbath" or "Sabbath Peace." The covering for the bread has its roots in the manna that the Children of Israel received in the desert as they wandered for 40 years. Dew would cover the manna every morning. As the dew covered the daily manna given by God, we cover the Sabbath bread today. Another less serious reason for the bread covering is to keep the bread from becoming "jealous" since the wine is chosen first to receive the blessing.

The blessing over the bread (called "*challah*" in Hebrew) is said by the father in the same manner as the blessing over the wine. There are usually two loaves of bread, although I do know some who adhere to the teaching from the book of Leviticus and have 12 loaves of bread on their table. The 12 loaves were what was required of the Israelites to be prepared for the Sabbath in order for the high priest to set them on the table in the Tabernacle before Almighty God (Leviticus 24:5-9). It is possible that these 12 loaves represent the 12 tribes of Israel. Either way, only two loaves are held together and the blessing is recited:

> *Blessed are you, O Lord our God, Creator of the universe, who brings forth bread from the earth.*

The two loaves of bread ("*challot*", plural of "*challah*" in Hebrew) remind everyone around the table of the double portion of manna that God gave the Israelites on the sixth day while they traveled in the desert for forty years.

The father then begins to cut or break the bread so that everyone can share in agreement with the stated blessing. The bread is usually sprinkled with salt or dipped in salt before being eaten. This is taken from the command given to the people of Israel to season every offering with salt, which is found in Leviticus 2:13. Religious Jews generally see the table in their home as a sort of altar since the Temple in Jerusalem is not standing today. As a result of this many of the offerings commanded in the Torah are reinterpreted and practiced in different ways. The use of salt with the bread is one of those examples.

The Reality of the Sabbath

The traditional Sabbath meal on Friday evening is filled with activity that could keep any family engaged until bed time. Since there is generally no use of the television or anything else like this in a religious Jewish home on Friday evening, what better way to spend the evening than to remember God's promises to His people and to enjoy time with family, friends, and loved ones?

I have included two resources at the end of this chapter for your consideration. The first resource is a schedule which documents the flow of a traditional Jewish Sabbath. The second resource contains a list of typical Jewish blessings as I have explained earlier. Should one desire to incorporate any or some of these blessings into the Sabbath commencement, these resources will be helpful.

We have looked in detail at the way religious Jews traditionally begin their Sabbath. The next step is to decide how your particular family will commence your own Sabbath day celebration.

A Traditional Schedule for the Sabbath

Sabbath Eve

- **Lighting of the Candles:** at least 18 minutes before sunset
- **Commencement of the Sabbath:** at the setting of the sun
- **Welcoming the Sabbath:** (at the synagogue) Psalm 29, 92-93, & 95-99
- **Sabbath Songs/Blessings:** (at home)
    - "Peace Unto You" ("*Shalom Aleichem*") Psalm 91
    - "An Excellent Wife" ("*Eshet Hayil*") Proverbs 31:10-31
    - Blessing of children (see "Blessings" schedule)
    - General blessing – Numbers 6:24-26
    - *Kiddush* – Genesis 1:31-2:3
    - Blessing over the wine (see "Blessings" schedule)
    - Blessing over the hands (see "Blessings" schedule)
    - Blessing over the bread (see "Blessings" schedule)
- **The Feast: The First Meal**
- **Activities for the Feast:**
    - Torah discussion
    - Psalms/Songs
    - Giving Thanks after the meal

Sabbath Day

- **Morning Worship**
- **Prelude to the Second Meal**
    - *Kiddush*: blessing over the wine
    - Blessing over the hands
    - Blessing over the bread (with salt)
- **The Second Meal**
- **Activities for the Second Meal**

- Torah discussion
- Psalms/Songs – Psalm 24
- Giving Thanks after the meal

- **Rest or Afternoon Activities**
- **Afternoon Prayer**
- **The Third Meal**
- **Evening Prayer & Conclusion of the Sabbath: *"Havdalah"***
- **Greeting the New Week**

Traditional Jewish Blessings

Candles:

Blessed are you, O Lord our God, King of the universe,
who has made us holy in His commandments
and commanded us to light the candles of the Sabbath.

Children:

Blessing over a son:
May God make you like Ephraim and Manasseh!
Blessing over a daughter:
May God make you like Sarah, Rebecca, Rachel, and Leah.

General Blessing:

The LORD bless you and keep you;
The LORD make His face shine on you,
And be gracious toward you:
The LORD lift up His countenance on you,
And give you peace. (Numbers 6:24-26)

Wine:

Blessed are you, O Lord our God, King of the universe,
Creator of the fruit of the vine.

Hands:

Blessed are you, O Lord our God, King of the universe,
who has made us holy by His commandments
and commanded us concerning the washing of the hands.

Bread:

Blessed are you, O Lord our God, Creator of the universe,
who brings forth bread from the earth.

Chapter 6

The Creation of Your Sabbath: The Foundation

The wise woman builds her house,...
Proverbs 14:1

Making the transition from the regular work week to the day of rest will set the foundation for the Sabbath. It is important to be intentional about beginning the Sabbath, which should be agreeable with all the members of the family. The activities that your family includes in the commencement of your day of rest should be prepared ahead of time and should enable all the family members to participate in one way or another.

The details in the last chapter provide a framework from which to begin to create one's own Sabbath day commencement. The main aspects to this framework include: an official time in which to begin, symbols of the Sabbath (candles, bread, wine, etc...), family blessings, songs, prayers, and the "*kiddush*," which is a traditional prayer in which the day is set apart unto God. It is important to understand that the traditional Jewish practices are given as a guide and are not intended to be viewed as an absolute standard. Use them as a base to create your own family traditions in keeping with the needs of your unique family. Used in this way, they will help provide a framework and direction for your Sabbath celebration.

Practical Applications

When to begin

You may choose a beginning for your Sabbath in the morning, afternoon or evening. If you do choose to start your day of rest according to the setting of the sun, there are numerous ways to calculate this. In our day and age the sun's setting and rising are listed in any local newspaper or can easily be found on a website for a certain city, town, or region. The important aspect of setting a proper time to begin is so that everyone involved in the Sabbath meal is ready at the proper hour. All the necessary preparations are made beforehand so that there may be an attitude of peaceful anticipation.

I recommend starting your day of rest in the afternoon or evening, because I believe it is easier for most people to come together at these hours rather than in the morning hours. Many Christians may view the start of their day of rest as Sunday morning. If this is the time that your family chooses to begin your Sabbath day, you must be sure to coordinate well and have everything finished on Saturday evening. If your family attends a weekly worship time on Sunday morning, your day of rest may begin before or after your worship time. If you choose to have an elaborate commencement including a meal as described in the last chapter, you may find it easier to commence your Sabbath day after your morning worship time, over brunch or lunch. Another idea is to begin your Sabbath time on Saturday evening. Starting the Sabbath in the evening will give your family the opportunity to have a full day together enjoying Sabbath rest.

The beginning time of the Sabbath needs to be chosen and communicated well. I learned in a business course I took with a wise professor that one must say everything at least three times because people do not usually understand the first time. Choose a time in which to begin your Sabbath and communicate it clearly to all those involved.

The Candles

Having at least two candles is a tradition that is a good idea and provides a pleasant atmosphere for the meal, especially if it is in the evening. The recitation of a prayer or blessing accompanying the lighting of the candles is optional. If you want to include the traditional blessing, the woman of the home should light the candles and say the blessing sometime before the start of the meal. If there is no woman in the home, a male can light them and say the blessing.

As with all the blessings in this chapter and in the chapters to come, feel free to use them or not use them as best suits your unique family or community situation. A short personal prayer thanking God for the Sabbath as one lights the candles is quite adequate and can be much more meaningful than simply repeating a traditional prayer. It is customary to not ask God for something specific during the Sabbath. Rather, we are to simply acknowledge Him as the Creator and Giver of all things. A prayer expressing gratitude is therefore very fitting for this occasion.

Songs & Blessings

The songs that are sung in the Jewish tradition are mostly Scripture adapted to a certain tune. I would encourage those of you who hope to make the Sabbath practice a family tradition to write your own songs. Use the book of Psalms in the Bible or simply write your own poetry regarding the Sabbath. The

Sabbath should be a festive time and you can make it as unique as you like with your own songs.

In a family situation the family blessings may be adopted and adapted as desired. The word benediction simply means "good" (bene) "words" (diction). The concept of speaking good words into the lives of other people is incredibly valuable. Below are several examples of the value of words from the book of Proverbs in the Bible:

There is one who speaks rashly like the thrusts of a sword,
but the tongue of the wise brings healing. (12:18)

A soothing tongue is a tree of life,
But perversion in it crushes the spirit. (15:4)

Pleasant words are a honeycomb,
Sweet to the soul and healing to the bones. (16:24)

Death and life are in the power of the tongue,
And those who love it will eat its fruit. (18:21)

When we are speaking "pleasant words" to each other it truly is health to our bodies. In my opinion, many medical practices would be obsolete if we simply learned to speak pleasant words to each other more often.

There are many ways to use and apply what I have shared here regarding the Jewish tradition of blessing different family members. In the simplest form the father or man of the home is to take the lead and express good words to his wife and children. He may use the blessings provided in this chapter and he may also add things that may be more personal as well. Proverbs 31 is generally sung by those around the table. (In the Jewish home there is rarely a solo. Rather, there are songs that everyone sings together. It is generally the men who sing this song but the women may sing it as well.) Or if you prefer, the text from Proverbs 31 may simply be read by one person while everyone else listens.

The wife may also share good words with her husband and children. There may be special occasions when it is someone's birthday and everyone shares good words with whoever's birthday it is. When the parents have their anniversary the children may bless their parents. These are just some ideas to help incorporate the concept of blessing into your Sabbath. The important thing is to appropriate this concept of blessing others that you care about during your Sabbath time. An inspiring example of appropriating this idea of blessing others is given by a couple, Rob and Susan, and is explained in their personal Sabbath schedule at the end of this chapter.

For those in the non-traditional setting of community, these ideas may easily be transferred into your situation as well. Generally the host should take initiative in his or her home to bless those who have come to the table. The Scripture taken from Proverbs 31 may be read or sung as a reminder of a thankful husband to a virtuous wife. The blessing found in Numbers 6 may also be read or sung as a general blessing over all those present.

The Holy Bible is filled with verses that may be read as a blessing over different people as one sees fit. There may also be more specific blessings that you wish to bestow on those who are at your table for being diligent in whatever their sphere of influence is: i.e. at the office, in the classroom, on the jobsite or whatever the case may be. Again the important thing is to speak pleasant words into the lives of others, remembering that God is our Creator and we are grateful to Him for giving us family, friends, and community.

Blessings over the Wine & Bread

The blessings over the wine (or grape juice, the important element being "the fruit of the vine") and bread may easily be adopted and used just as they are traditionally. Or, you could make up your own blessings as you set this special day apart. There should be freedom to express ourselves to God in a respectful way and in a way that is genuine, not forced or "cookie cutter." Some of the best Sabbath meals I have attended have been when the host did something unique that was appropriate to the situation.

One particular Sabbath meal that I shared in while in Jerusalem was unforgettable! I was with a family that would be considered Orthodox from the Breslev division of Judaism. They are generally cheerful people that enjoy life, and this family was no different. The husband and wife are a dynamic couple and gifted hosts. The husband is a writer and has a seemingly endless vault from which to pull stories. All throughout the evening he recounted different anecdotes that related to the proceedings of the Sabbath and the topics we were discussing. Because his stories were intricately connected to the event for which we were gathered, the flow of the evening was especially fluid and dynamic. As this man stepped out of tradition, which could easily become merely ritualistic, he blessed his guests with a unique celebration of how the Sabbath is enjoyed in his home and how it is relevant to him and his family in our modern era. Be creative with your Sabbath blessings!

The Flow of the Sabbath:

Creating your own unique Sabbath experience may not be easy. However, with intentional effort and a lot of working together in unity a memorable time will be enjoyed by all. To help guide you through the course of the evening of the Sabbath and the following day, three schedules have been included at the end of this chapter. The first one is a simple schedule for the Sabbath day which provides an outline of events. The second one provides an example schedule of how one couple developed their own effective Sabbath day of rest within their community. They begin their celebration on Saturday afternoon and end it on Sunday afternoon. The third schedule details how a traditional Jewish couple with twelve children lives out the Sabbath in their home with each member contributing something. There is also an additional schedule at the end of Chapter 11 that provides a general overview of the course of the week. These schedules may be followed or deviated from as you desire and as is suitable to your particular family or community.

Though a great deal of possible structure has thus far been provided, it is important to remember that this structure is intended only as a guide. It is my desire that you take all that you learn and create a unique Sabbath day experience in community with family and friends in a way that produces joy and life. Aside from not working and not lighting a fire, not much is included in the biblical text concerning the Sabbath. Be imaginative and develop a Sabbath of your very own!

New Testament Connections

There are some interesting parallels in the New Testament that should be noted here and given some thought.

1. As we have discussed, the use of candles on the Sabbath is a reminder of how God commanded His people to remember the Sabbath day and keep it holy. They are also a reminder of God's command in the Old Testament to keep the lamp burning before Him in the Temple. In the New Testament Jesus refers to Himself as "the light of the world" (John 8:12); for Christians, therefore, there may be this added symbolism of the candles representing Jesus, as well.

2. The bread and the wine are also very important in the New Testament teachings. Most Christians will automatically think of the communion service that is practiced weekly or monthly in their church. Jesus gave this practice to His disciples before He was arrested and crucified. During a Passover celebration with His disciples Jesus sanctified Himself before His disciples by taking the bread and wine and shared it with His disciples. Let us look at this event directly from the text.

> *And when He had taken some bread and given thanks, He broke it, and gave it to them saying, 'This is My body which is given for you; do this in remembrance of Me.' And in the same way He took the cup after they had eaten saying; 'This cup which is poured out for you is the new covenant in My blood.' (Luke 22:19-20)*

This is a very accurate picture of Jesus who, being Jewish, took something from tradition as well as from the Passover ceremony to explain to His disciples that He was Someone who was sanctified and set apart unto God for a specific purpose. He also commissioned His followers to continually take the cup of wine and eat the bread as a reminder of what He would do for them by dying on the cross.

I know some Christians who like to practice the Sabbath using the Jewish traditions and to incorporate the weekly "Communion" service during the commencement of the Sabbath when they drink the wine and eat the bread. This is certainly an option. However, I do not believe the sanctifying of the Sabbath as a day set apart and the practice of communion must go hand in hand for Christians.

The practice of the Sabbath is an event that uses the age-old tradition of setting something apart unto God by using the bread and wine. As I mentioned earlier in this chapter, this practice goes back to Abraham and Melchizedek. In understanding Jesus' act of sanctifying Himself with the wine and bread as the basis of instituting the communion service, one can see the connection between the two (the sanctifying act and the communion service) and still appreciate them as separate entities. Those with whom you celebrate the Sabbath must decide how to handle the understanding of the wine and the bread in your Sabbath celebration as Christians. The wine and bread may either be used as a sanctifying act for a special day alone or as a combination of both the sanctifying act and as a remembrance of the death, burial, and resurrection of Jesus.

3. Taking the bread by itself, it is interesting to note that in the New Testament Jesus makes reference to Himself as bread. Jesus said *"I am the bread of life; he who comes to Me shall not hunger, and he who believes in Me shall never thirst"* (John 6:35). The sanctity of the bread can be appreciated more as Christians reflect on these words of Jesus before they partake of the bread.

4. Another unique tie-in found in the New Testament is related to the washing of the hands. As mentioned earlier, there is an interesting and mysterious double meaning within the Hebrew word for washing, incorporating both "washing" and "lifting." In Psalm 24 there is a reference to having clean hands before God. In answering the question of who may ascend the hill of the LORD and stand in His holy place, the text reads, *"He who has clean hands and a pure heart..."* (24:4). Clean hands mentioned here infer a requirement which goes beyond physical presentation into spiritual condition.

There is also a verse in the New Testament that refers to lifting up hands. Paul wrote the following to Timothy in one of his letters:

Therefore I want the men in every place to pray, lifting up holy hands, without wrath and dissension. (1 Timothy 2:8)

It may be helpful for Christians to focus on this verse when considering or performing the act of washing one's hands before the blessing over the bread. God wants His people to be holy and this does not only mean having clean hands physically but also clean hands spiritually before God.

This focus of maintaining proper priorities is brought up by Jesus Himself. In Matthew Chapter 15 the Pharisees and scribes asked Jesus why His disciples transgressed the traditions of the elders by not washing their hands when they ate bread (v.1-2). Jesus responded by asking the Pharisees why they transgressed the commands of God for the sake of their traditions (v.3) and continued to give them an example regarding how they dishonored their own parents (v.4-6). In this same context, Jesus explained to His disciples that matters of the heart are more important than washed hands. Later in this chapter, Jesus explains His rebuke of the Pharisees to His disciples:

For out of the heart comes evil thoughts, murders, adulteries, fornications, thefts, false witness, slanders. These are the things which defile the man; but to eat with unwashed hands does not defile the man. (v.19-20)

Jesus is not advocating unsanitary conditions in food handling but simply focusing on the more important issues. Jesus was pointing out to the Pharisees that the traditions of men must never invalidate the commands of God. Jesus also explained to His disciples that to have a clean heart before God is more important than washed hands.

Therefore, the next time you have a meal, whether it is a

Sabbath meal or not, take time to consider your spiritual condition. People can see the dirt on our hands and we can wash that away with water but only God sees the dirt in our hearts and He alone can make the spiritual heart clean.

A Simple Schedule for the Sabbath

Some Evening:

- **An official time in which to begin**
- **A special meal with several courses**
- **Activities throughout the meal to keep everyone involved**
    - Discussion of a certain topic (with a spiritual basis)
    - Opportunity for each one to share about their week
    - A selected story for children
    - Giving of thanks for the meal and time together

The Following Day:

- **A Morning Worship Time**
- **The Second Meal:** Late morning brunch/lunch
- **Afternoon Activities**
    - Play games together
    - Outdoor activities:
      Go for a walk, hike, bike ride
      Go to a park
      Play a sport
- **Evening Meal**
- **Conclusion of the Sabbath, *"Havdalah"***
- **Greeting the New Week**

Example Schedule for the Sabbath #1

This schedule is taken from a married couple, Rob & Susan, who have read this book and have developed a Sabbath day of their own. Their Sabbath begins at one o'clock in the afternoon on Saturday and goes to one o'clock in the afternoon on Sunday as fits their schedules best.

Saturday Afternoon

- The Sabbath begins at 1pm and a prayer is said welcoming the Sabbath.
- After the prayer until the Sabbath guests arrive, Susan is usually preparing the meal, setting the table, and finishing up the last-minute details.
- Two candles are lit shortly before the guests arrive in the afternoon/evening.

Saturday Evening

- The *"Rock Ceremony"* – After the guests have arrived and are seated at the table, they are invited to think on "the rock" (which symbolizes a burden, something that took their focus off of God, or something that stole their joy away during the week). Each person at the table is invited to write that burden on a rock and place it into a basket. A prayer is then prayed giving up that particular burden to God and asking Him to remove that "rock" out of their lives. Rob and Susan keep the rocks so that they can pray for the burdens of their friends and look for a Scripture during the week to replace the burdens with God's promises.
- Rob offers a prayer of thanksgiving. Then Rob pours a glass of wine for everyone and says a blessing over the wine. In like manner Rob says a blessing over the

bread and gives a piece to everyone at the table. (Blessings taken from Luke 22:17-20)

- Dinner officially begins and continues over a five or six-course meal:
    - soup, salad, an appetizer, the main course, fruit & nuts, and then dessert with coffee & tea.
- During dinner there is conversation about "the rocks" or about something good that God has done in the lives of those present during the week. Guests are invited to share a favorite scripture, such as a Psalm.
- Sometime during or after the appetizer, there is a blessing of one another with good words. They call it ***"What I Love About You."*** Before the guests arrive, Susan prays for each guest and focuses on what she loves or admires about each one. She writes a little note that details this. Then she rolls it up, ties it with a ribbon, and places it on the table. During the meal Susan opens each note, reads it to the person, and gives it to them. Then each person has the opportunity to share what they like, love, or admire about each person at the table (if they wish).
- After dinner they spend time together talking and then close with prayer.

Sunday Morning

- Rob & Susan go to church or simply listen to a sermon online.
- They eat brunch which is made up of leftovers.
- Their Sabbath ends at about one o'clock in the afternoon and Rob leaves for work.

Example Schedule for the Sabbath #2

This schedule is from a married couple, Adam & Rachel, with twelve children who have developed a Sabbath day of their own. They hold to a more traditional Sabbath as Messianic Jews by keeping it from sunset to sunset on Friday and Saturday.

Preparation for the Sabbath:

- Adam works a fulltime job but only works a half day on Friday so that he can prepare himself for the Sabbath. He and his wife have chosen to educate their children at home and they use Friday as preparation day for the Sabbath.
- Everyone helps out with the preparations on Friday. The house is swept, clothes are washed and ironed, bathrooms are cleaned, and the little boys are bathed.
- The refrigerator is cleaned out early on Friday and all the leftovers are consumed to make room for the fresh Sabbath food.
- One of the daughters bakes the *challah* bread and the girls make sure the table is set with candles and clean *kiddush* cups.
- All the food is prepared during the day on Friday. A staple meal for the Sabbath includes a turkey (two if guests are invited) or chicken (four of them), mashed potatoes, rice, cabbage, and stuffing.
- Before sunset, on Friday, Adam gives each of the children their weekly allowance. They in turn take 10% and put it in a *pushke* (offering box) for *tzedakah* (tithe/alms for the poor). When the *pushke* is full, the children vote on where they want to send the money.

Friday Evening: Welcoming the Sabbath

- To greet the Sabbath, Rachel and each of the girls light their own candles and recite the blessing.
- They sing a special Sabbath song and exchange hugs.
- Adam then reads a short portion from the Torah and they sing the traditional song *"Vezot HaTorah"* (This is the Torah). And they all kiss the Torah out of respect for God's Word.
- They sing a few songs, either traditional Sabbath songs like *Shalom Aleichem* or Messianic songs. They always include a special song about returning to Israel one day; Adam takes the three youngest boys one by one and places them on his shoulders and dances around the table as the boys wave goodbye to their siblings.
- Adam blesses each of his children individually and then reads Proverbs 31 as a way of blessing his wife. Rachel in turn recites Psalm 112 as a blessing to Adam.
- Adam recites the Aaronic blessing over his children.
- Adam and the boys perform the kiddush and say the blessing over the *challah* bread and then they start the meal.
- During dinner, Adam asks the question, "Who remembers this week's Torah portion?" There are a wide variety of responses ranging from the little ones to the older ones. The Torah portion is discussed during the meal.
- Adam reads a story for the younger children and then a commentary for the adults relating to the Torah portion.
- After the meal is finished they sing the *"Birkat Hamazon"* (Blessing for the food).
- The girls talk to one another and Adam, if he is still awake, tells the boys a story.

Saturday Morning: Worship

- Breakfast is traditionally fresh fruit and cottage cheese.
- The family worship time is comprised of reading the Torah and Haftorah readings along with a chapter from the gospels. They have discussion after each reading.
- There may be another family that joins them for this discussion in the morning.

Saturday Afternoon: Activities/Rest

- Lunch usually consists of tuna sandwiches or, if there are leftovers, they have chicken or turkey sandwiches.
- Adam sometimes goes for a leisurely walk with the children down the country road or through the orchard.

Saturday Evening: Closing the Sabbath

- Adam and the boys lead the family in a traditional *"Havdalah"* ceremony to bring the Sabbath to an end and to greet the new week.

Chapter 7

The Head of the Sabbath: The Feast

Go then, eat your bread in happiness, and
drink your wine with a cheerful heart;
for God has already approved your works.
Ecclesiastes 9:7

One day I was talking to a friend about the Sabbath and how I enjoy practicing it in community. We talked about joining his family and some other friends so that everyone could experience and understand the Sabbath first hand. Since he is not Jewish, the whole concept of practicing the Sabbath was a bit foreign to him, although he was interested in learning more. We set a time on a Friday evening in order to enjoy some of the traditions of a Sabbath meal together.

As Friday evening drew closer we began to discuss the details of the dinner and the flow of the evening. As we talked, he began to have reservations concerning people in his home for this dinner combined with a discussion about the Sabbath. He asked me, "What's so important about this meal? Couldn't we just get together and you could talk about the Sabbath without the meal?" To him the "Sabbath meal" was simply a dinner that preceded our discussion about a religious topic. To me, it was like he was saying, "Couldn't we just have Thanksgiving without the turkey, the mashed potatoes, and the pumpkin pie?"

The Sabbath meal on Friday evening is the "kick off" for the rest of the game which takes place in the twenty four hours that follow. If one lives in the United States, an evening meal may last no more than half an hour. During the remainder of the evening different family members may either sit in front of the computer or television. They may read a book, or engage in whatever else may catch their attention. Having spent a few years now in the Middle East I have come to learn to enjoy a meal that typically lasts for several hours.

Jewish Tradition

The Feast

After the initial blessings and songs, during the evening of the Sabbath, the meal is served. Wine is generally served along with the meal and, depending on one's personal convictions, "Le Hayim"s ("toasts," literally translated "To Life!") are made throughout the night. The goal is not to get drunk. In fact, in the religious Jewish community it is generally looked upon as shameful to get drunk, and self-control is strongly encouraged. The goal is to enjoy the evening. As my father always says, "All things in moderation." If one prefers not to have alcohol, grape juice may be substituted.

In Israel, it is fairly common to have several courses during the Sabbath meal. These include soup, different dips/sauces (for example: hummus) that are served with bread, different salads, an appetizer of fish, the main dish or dishes (generally a chicken dish, a beef dish, or both) with various hot vegetables, and then dessert. I have had meals in Israel that have so many courses I lost count.

On one occasion I went to a family's house with a couple of friends of mine for a Sabbath meal. After all of the initial appetizers, soup, and fish, we enjoyed several different kinds of salads with chicken in them. Then there was a tray served with different kinds of meat. I assumed this had to be the last dish since I was full before the tray of meats even came around. That was not the case, because soon after we finished that dish they brought out the "Cholent," which is a traditional Jewish Sabbath dish made with meat, beans, and potatoes. Despite my reputation for having a healthy appetite, I was not able to even take a bite.

There is no real right or wrong way to prepare your Sabbath meal. If you ask ten different Jewish mothers you will surely get eleven different ideas about which foods to prepare. There is a great deal of diversity because Jews have been scattered all over the world and have adopted various foods and customs from as far even as the Far East.

As mentioned above, one common food generally served as an appetizer on the Sabbath is fish. This is because in the Genesis account of the creation God blessed three things after he created them: Fish, Man, and the Sabbath. Therefore, it has become tradition that on the **Sabbath, Man** is to eat **Fish**, thereby incorporating all three blessings. It also seems that God blessed the birds of the sky when he blessed the fish but this has not yet caught on as a typical Jewish tradition, although chicken is a staple meat served on the Sabbath.

Songs/Psalms during the Meal

As I have previously mentioned, the meal is not an island unto itself and should not be separated from the activity of the evening. It is integrated into the whole practice of the Sabbath. In a traditional Jewish home the evening meal can easily last for several hours, though this is by no means mandatory. There are hundreds, if not thousands, of songs to choose from and at different times of the year there are certain favorites, depending on the holiday that surrounds that particular Sabbath. These songs are generally sung between the different courses. Many times the father or leader of the home will be the one who chooses a song or he may simply ask if anyone has a suggestion and that person leads as everyone joins in.

There is also a unique and special compilation of songs called "*Zemirot*" (or *zmirot*) that are traditionally sung during the meal. These songs have been added over the course of time and have become a type of dinner hymnal for the Sabbath. For each song there are a number of different tunes to which that particular song can be sung. These songs (or poems) have become traditional in the Jewish home and generally those around the table are familiar with them.

Torah Discussion during the Meal

Another key activity during the meal is a discussion of the Torah portion of the week. The Torah (the first five books of the Jewish and Christian Bibles) is read from beginning to end every Hebrew calendar year and the chapters and verses are broken into fifty four sections, each consisting of a few chapters. There are fifty four sections because in the Hebrew calendar there is a leap month once every few years. The sections are apportioned according to the weeks of the year but at times some sections need to be doubled so that the readings are completed by the end of the year. Each of these sections is studied in turn throughout the week by men, women, and children. The section of the week is then read in its entirety in the local synagogue on the morning of the Sabbath, Saturday morning. There are also supplemental readings (Haftorah readings) usually taken from the Prophets that connect in some way with the Torah portion. The Torah portion of the week is a fundamental element to the evening meal for religious Jews.

Just as there is a great assortment of foods to choose from and songs to be sung, so there are also numerous ways that the Torah portion can be included in the evening meal. In some homes the Torah portion is read around the table before or after the main meal. This method allows all to participate in reading as well as sharing the honor of proclaiming God's Word. Sometimes one person is given the task of summarizing the Torah portion for all those around the table. He or she then shares any pertinent life lessons that they have learned as they have studied the text that week. In many families, each one will have opportunity to share with the others what really stood out to them about that particular portion of Scripture or simply what they liked about it. This is generally called "Davar Torah" meaning "a word of Torah" or more literally, "a word of teaching." The focal point during this part of the Sabbath is to remember God's Word and to talk about how it applies to life.

Giving Thanks

The traditions of the blessings over the wine and the bread are the introduction to the Sabbath meal, and just as there is an introduction there is closure. Religious Jews generally give thanks to God for their meal after they have finished eating and it is no different on the Sabbath. This tradition comes from Deuteronomy 8:10 and following where Moses instructs the Israelites:

> *When you have eaten and are satisfied, you shall bless the LORD your God for the good land which He has given you.*

Therefore, Orthodox Jewish people say a blessing after they have eaten, in order to remember God and praise His name, having satisfied themselves with food.

There are many particular blessings said by religious Jews, according to the food which is eaten. However, on the Sabbath, there is a unique blessing that is read after each of the meals. This special blessing is called *"Birkat Hamazon"* meaning "the blessing of the food." It is a very long and detailed prayer that praises God for all that He is and all He has done for His people. Specifically, it thanks Him for how He has brought them out of slavery and into a good and spacious land, the Land of Israel. This blessing also includes prayers for one's family (parents), the host of the meal, and for all of those present. Actually, this blessing is uttered after any given meal during the week at which bread is eaten. However, there are some special additions to this blessing which are read only on the Sabbath. For example, on the Sabbath Psalm 126 is sung or read as an introduction to the regular body of the blessing. The entire prayer is very comprehensive and much too long to include here; however, it can easily be found on the World Wide Web (*"Birkat Hamazon"* or in English "Grace After Meals") or by perusing Jewish books on Sabbath practice.

Cleanup after the Meal

The meal and activities which are intertwined during the evening eventually come to an end and then reality sets in. After dinner the table is cleared and the dishes are brought to the kitchen. How is cleanup handled on the Sabbath?

Religious Jews will typically follow the rules set down by their rabbi. Some will let the dishes pile up until after the Sabbath while others will use plastic plates and eating utensils that can simply be thrown into the trash. Most religious Jews, with whom I have personally spent time, use real plates and silverware. After the meal they do a general cleanup; put food away, get rid of trash, and at least rinse the plates and silverware in order to keep food from becoming caked on. They will then wash all the dishes after the Sabbath has ended.

Practical Applications

The Meal

There are no specific commands in the Bible as to what foods to eat on the Sabbath, so there is much freedom to be enjoyed. The important thing is to have a meal, whether it is breakfast, lunch or dinner, that you will enjoy with your family and will provide more than enough for everyone to eat (if this is possible). There are plenty of Jewish cookbooks for those who want more ideas. One book that I can recommend is titled *Simply Israel* by T. Gila Levine. I have enjoyed a few of the selections contained in this book, as prepared by the author herself, and know that the recipes therein are a true taste of Israel.

Songs During the Meal

For those who want to participate in a more traditional Jewish style Sabbath evening with the traditional songs, there is a plethora of materials on the market. For those who want a simple English-Hebrew booklet with prayers, blessings, and a variety of songs, there are booklets called "Benchers" that I have found to be a great asset. It must be kept in mind that these booklets are made for Jews and assume that the reader knows how to use them. There is not much explanation in the booklet and they are generally written in Hebrew with English translation. There are also CDs on the market for those who want to learn the Sabbath songs in Hebrew and wish to teach them to their family.

For those who want a less traditional Sabbath evening and want to tweak it to your situation, there are plenty of ways to do this. One way is to sing songs with which you and your family are already familiar. Songs about the greatness of God, man's dependence on God, or simply songs about resting are a good place to start. If practicing the Sabbath is new for you and your family, you may find certain members overwhelmed by all of the new activity. Incorporating as many familiar things as you are able will add to a level of comfort. The focus of this time is simply to celebrate the Sabbath, a day of rest which God has given us to enjoy.

An alternative to the *Zemirot* and the traditional songs sung during the meal is to read certain verses from the Bible, especially the Psalms. The Psalms are filled with short chapters of praise that help us focus on God. They emphasize God as the King of all creation. Invite someone around your table to read a Psalm. Afterward ask them to explain why they chose that particular Psalm, what can be learned about God, and how it can be applied to real life.

The Torah Portion – "God's Word"

As you read this book there may be some new language that is possibly unfamiliar. "Torah portion" may be an example of this. "Torah portion" in simplest terms is a few chapters taken from the Torah that are read and studied week by week and linked to another portion of Scripture taken from the rest of the Old Testament Scriptures, usually from the Prophets. This additional section is called the "Haftorah." The Torah portion together with the Haftorah is the traditional way that Jews study the Scriptures, God's Word!

There are many references to the "Torah portion" found in the New Testament. One example of this is found in Luke Chapter 24. It was the first day of the week, the day Jesus was resurrected. Two of the disciples of Jesus were walking along the road to Emmaus, a village outside of Jerusalem. Jesus joined them on the journey to Emmaus and asked them about the things they were discussing along the way. The two disciples were prevented from recognizing Him and one of them began to explain how they were struggling to understand all that had happened to this prophet from Nazareth named Jesus. They explained that they had hoped that He would redeem Israel but instead He was delivered up to be crucified by the religious rulers. Even more disturbing was what they had heard that very morning, that some of the women amongst them had actually been to the tomb and said that they had seen angels who told them that Jesus had risen from the dead. As they stood perplexed about all these things, Jesus said to them:

> *O foolish men and slow of heart to believe in all that the prophets have spoken! Was it not necessary for the Christ to suffer these things and to enter into His glory? And beginning with Moses and with all the prophets, He explained to them the things concerning Himself in all the Scriptures. (Luke 24:25-27)*

They eventually arrived at their destination in Emmaus and Jesus revealed Himself to them over dinner and then disappeared from their sight. The two disciples were amazed at this encounter with Jesus.

"Moses and the Prophets" as referred to by Jesus in the above Scripture are the essence of "The Torah Portion" along with the "Haftorah." The very method used by the Jews in Jesus' day and used by Jesus Himself is the same method that Jewish people use today to study the Scriptures. Jesus used this method to explain to these two disciples how His death and resurrection were fulfillments of Old Testament prophecies. The Torah portion represents God's Word, and the Jews have developed a very organized way in which to read through the Torah each year with connections throughout the Old Testament.

If you choose to integrate the Torah portion into your Sabbath meal, I would suggest appointing someone to give a summary of it and comment on one or two of the highlights that they would like to share with everyone else. Others can be given the chance to share their insights on this section of Scripture as well. In this way everyone learns from one another and is reminded of God's faithfulness to His people. We need all the help we can get in this world in which we live today, especially for the family.

Although the Torah portion is usually discussed during the meal, it can easily be something that is done after the meal. I have done it both ways and both work well. A list detailing how the Torah portions are broken up by chapter and verse is found toward the end of this book as a supplement. However, in order to find the current Torah portion (along with the accompanying Haftorah reading) for a certain week, one will have to surf the internet or obtain a schedule from a local synagogue.

Another option for the Torah portion during the Sabbath is to have some type of Bible study from some other portion of the Bible (Old or New Testaments) and have a discussion about what is shared. This is not meant to be a sermon but something short, perhaps from five to ten minutes, followed by a discussion. The Jewish Torah portion provides a ready made schedule to read and study the Bible week by week, but this is not the only way. There are unlimited ways to study God's Word and provide spiritual nourishment during your Sabbath experience. The important element in the Torah portion segment of the Sabbath is to provide spiritual food that is shared among all of those who are participating in this day of rest and restoration.

Giving Thanks

The giving of thanks at the conclusion of the meal is a good reminder to all those present that all that was eaten was from the hand of God. I encourage you to do this as it is a good practice to give thanks, remember the family in prayer, and to bless the host or hostess. This may be done in different ways. In a Jewish setting one person usually prays and everyone else listens, or sometimes all of those present at the table pray at the same time since they are praying the same words. In the Christian setting generally one person prays only at the beginning of the meal and everyone listens in agreement. The important thing here is that there is a thankful spirit after everyone has finished eating. It also provides closure to the meal itself. People may continue to sit around the table and drink tea or coffee, but the meal itself has come to an end.

Reality Check: More *Cay*?

There are so many ways to be creative with an Erev Shabbat meal. Some may like structure and want every minute planned out. Others will prefer to "wing it" and simply have a good time with family and friends. Whichever way you choose to practice the Sabbath, let the focus always be on the Creator God who has given us life and on the family and friends that He has given us with whom to enjoy the Sabbath. With this in mind I would like to share a story, reminding you to set your watch aside and to enjoy the evening with the people you are surrounded by.

I have always enjoyed drinking tea. I begin my day with a couple of glasses of green tea in the morning and have been doing so for many years. While I was living and working in Istanbul I would drink tea all day long and into the night because it is very much a part of the culture there. When someone offers you a glass of tea it is a way of saying, "Sit down, stay a while, and let's talk." Schedules and meetings are not as important as friendship, and this is demonstrated by taking the time to set the schedule aside and drink a glass of tea together.

Turkish hospitality is typical of the Middle East. Guests are always honored and the best of whatever one can afford is set before them. In Istanbul, when I went to a friend's home for a meal I would generally arrive between 6 and 7 in the evening, and the earliest I would arrive home would be after midnight. As a general rule I ate or drank something from the moment I walked in the door until just before putting on my jacket to leave. What did we do for five or six hours?

For the most part we had a meal as is common in most countries around the world. We had soup, salad, some different side dishes and the main course. The basic meal was over within the first couple of hours of arriving. However, an important element came next and that was the *cay*! The word for tea in Turkish is "*cay*" (pronounced "chai"). Turkish *cay* is a type of black tea. The pot of water went on the stove right after dinner was finished and *cay* was served throughout the evening and into the night. We would have a glass of *cay* as we sat and talked. We had some more *cay* as we had our dessert of baklava or something of this sort. After dessert we had more *cay*. The discussion continued as long as the *cay* held out. As soon as I had finished a glass of *cay* my host or hostess offered me another glass of *cay* before the glass had even gotten cold. It was considered shameful not to continually offer a guest *cay*. While I lived in Istanbul I learned that going to someone's home for a meal was not going to be a quick hour or two and then on to my next appointment. Along with the meal came lots of *cay* and with *cay* came relationship.

Relationship is something that can easily be missed in western society today. Personally, I do not believe that a meal should consist only of food that is apportioned to each person. Rather, I believe that a meal should include a time to share with others, including the children. Whether it takes tea, coffee, hot cocoa, or some other type of hot or cold drink, take the time to enjoy the company of others (especially the family) over a festive meal at least once a week. Hence the Sabbath meal!

Cleanup after the Meal

Though this component of the Sabbath may seem trivial to some of you, cleanup is a reality, especially for mothers. If the process of cleaning up is not organized in an efficient way, the Sabbath experience can become more of a nightmare than an oasis in time.

For those who enjoy a consistent Sabbath, it is best to have a set method in which cleanup after the meals is handled. Perhaps one may choose to follow the religious Jewish practice and leave the dishes until after the Sabbath or use plastic plates and utensils. Nevertheless, one or two people need to be responsible to clean off the table, dispose of trash, and put food away. If real dishes are used, one may choose to have them totally cleaned after the meal either by hand or with the help of a dishwasher. One or two people need to be appointed to this responsibility before the Sabbath begins so that they are prepared to carry this out. No one likes surprise responsibilities placed on them. Whether your community is in a family setting or in some other setting of community, clear communication in this area of clean up will help everyone involved in the Sabbath celebration enjoy the day more fully.

There is much flexibility and personal choice in this area of cleanup. I believe each family or community needs to thoughtfully consider this issue and decide what works best for them. Perhaps a rotating schedule may be implemented so that the duties of cleanup do not always fall on the mother of the home. The important thing is to have a clear plan in mind and to communicate it effectively.

New Testament Connections

The Torah portion can easily be connected to the New Testament and be integrated into the Sabbath meal. Jesus and His apostles often refer to and quote from the Torah as well as from other sections of the Tanakh (the Jewish Bible or the Christian Old Testament), since this comprised their entire Bible at that time. I encourage the Christian reader to try to connect the Torah portion of the week with some portion of Scripture in the New Testament, whether the Torah portion is quoted in the New Testament or not.

I will give an example of this here to illustrate how this may be accomplished. I will take a few verses from the Torah portion found in Numbers 4:21- 7:89. In the beginning of this Torah portion there is a detailed rendering of the responsibilities of three clans from the tribe of Levi (4:21-49). God specifically tells Moses and Aaron to count the men from thirty to fifty years of age from these clans and to assign each clan specific jobs that were to be carried out in maintaining the Tabernacle. Aaron and his sons were to oversee this work as it was completed by specific men within specific clans. God had each man counted and assigned a specific job in the care of His Tabernacle. We understand from this that God is involved in and concerned about the details of life, especially as it involves worship of Him.

In the New Testament we can see a very similar pattern of God being involved in the details of those who believe in Him. After the resurrection and ascension of Jesus to heaven, the Holy Spirit is given to the believers as Jesus promised. The Apostle Paul speaks of the giving of the Holy Spirit in his letter to the Corinthians: "*But to each one is given the manifestation of the Spirit for the common good*" (1 Corinthians 12:7). Paul then continues to give a list of various spiritual gifts and how they are to work in unison.

In his letter to the Ephesians, Paul gives further insight as to the exact purpose of the spiritual gifts that God gives to believers in Jesus:

> *And He gave some as apostles, and some as prophets, and some as evangelists, and some as pastors and teachers, for the equipping of the saints for the work of service, to the building up of the body of Christ; until we all attain to the unity of the faith, and of knowledge of the Son of God, to a mature man, to the measure of the stature which belongs to the fullness of Christ. (Ephesians 4:11-13)*

In other words, God gives *specific* gifts to *specific* believers in Jesus to build up the different members of the greater community of believers so that there will be maturity and unity.

God's care for His children in both the Old and New Testaments is quite clear and very precise. God is involved in the way in which we worship Him and He desires for each person to know his or her responsibilities before Him and in relation to others. God is involved in the details of our lives.

There are many connections that may be made between the Torah portion and the New Testament. The more we examine this, the more we will discover the New Testament connections to the Torah and enjoy the spiritual focus of the discussions around the table.

Chapter 8

The Spirit of the Sabbath: WORSHIP

A Psalm, a Song for the Sabbath day.
IT is good to give thanks to the LORD,
And to sing praises to Thy name,
O Most High
Psalm 92:1

The meal welcoming the Sabbath on Friday evening is the highlight of the celebration for religious Jews. However, the meal is only the beginning of the Sabbath. We will now discuss Saturday which is the actual day of the Sabbath.

The Sabbath day for religious Jews is the true dividing line between the "holy" and the "secular." This is my considered opinion after living in Israel for some time. For religious Jews, the Sabbath is first and foremost a day to attend the synagogue, to pray, to recite the "Shema" (the Jewish creed) and to listen to the reading of the Torah portion. It is considered a privilege and an honor to be invited for an "aliyah" (to be called up to the front in order to be a witness to the reading of the Torah and to say a blessing). For the secular Jew, the Sabbath is a day to sleep in or possibly go on a daytrip with friends. Who has chosen the best? This is for you to decide.

Jewish Tradition

Sabbath Morning Worship

For the religious Jew, the "Erev Shabbat meal" is the start of the Sabbath or the "preview" to the coming event. The morning of the Sabbath at the synagogue could be considered the "main event" or the "feature presentation." At the synagogue the Torah portion is read in its entirety and all those attending listen to it in agreement. The "Haftorah" is then read after the Torah portion. There are also many songs, psalms, and prayers surrounding the reading of the Torah portion. Here is a list of typical prayers and readings included during a Sabbath morning worship time in a synagogue:

- **The Akeidah – On the morning of the Sabbath, just like everyday during the morning prayers, the Genesis 22 account of Abraham being tested to offer up his son on the altar is one of the many biblical excerpts that are part of the Jewish prayer book. This particular account is a beautiful reminder to be obedient to God, to walk by faith, and of God's faithfulness to those who heed His voice.**
- **Offerings – There is also a recalling of God's commandments concerning the offerings. Since the Temple is not standing today, Jews cannot present offerings at the Temple. Therefore, the offerings have become part of the daily prayers.**
- **Psalms – The reading or singing of the following Psalms: 19, 24, 29, 30, 33, 34, 90-93, 135, 136, & 145-150.**
- **The Shema – "Hear O Israel, the Lord your God, the Lord is One!" (Deut. 6:4). This creed is declared by everyone in the synagogue, and is considered to be a major tenet of Judaism.**

- **The Definition of Loving God – Deut. 6:5-9. These verses are prayed.**
- **The Torah Portion is read.**
- **The Haftorah Portion is read.**
- **The Priestly Blessing – Numbers 6:24-26. This blessing is recited upon the people by those who are descended from the Kohanim (the descendants of Aaron).**

The list above is not comprehensive nor is it identical in every synagogue. There are two main streams of Judaism, Ashkenazi and Sephardic, and within these two streams there are many variations. As a result of this diversity, there will be a different focus and emphasis in different synagogues according to the traditions of that particular group of Jewish people. The list above is the general flow from an Ashkenazi perspective. Jews from various backgrounds will incorporate the readings above in one way or another. They may add a different Psalm at some point or sing a different song. An example of this is that in a Sephardic synagogue, the entire book of the Song of Songs (The Song of Solomon) is generally sung during the Friday evening service at the synagogue. Ashkenazi Jews typically do not sing this song in the synagogue.

Many Jewish people view these practices as the way to obey God and seek to live a life in unity with Him. I did not grow up attending synagogue, yet I find within these practices a beautiful way to worship God and I learn something new each week. The Torah is an amazing book that is filled with lessons for life. I believe that a person could study the Torah portion every week from the time they were a child until old age and always find new riches contained within it. In fact, some rabbis have spoken about the "seventy facets of the Torah" and believe that each facet pertains to each year of a person's life.

There are parts of the Sabbath morning worship time that are repetitious and seem somewhat unexciting, but I have found that there are many hidden jewels in these ancient prayers and traditions. I personally never tire of reading the account of Abraham with Isaac (the "Akeidah") and recounting Abraham's faith in God, or the way God sends His angel at the very last second saving Abraham from taking his precious son's life. The chosen Psalms for the Sabbath are filled with wonderful truths as well. They recount God's power over the universe and remind us of who we are before Him. The Shema and the following verses, which remind us of how we are to love God, are timeless. I believe we need these regular reminders of how we are to live our lives. There are many more hidden treasures contained within the Sabbath service and each time we experience a service, we find another gem.

The Sabbath morning worship time for the religious Jew is about keeping one's focus on God. Tradition and repetition are the hallmarks of the service. Tradition is what typically marks the Jewish people. The key for a religious Jew is to never lose sight of God in the midst of the traditional aspects of worship. Worship should always be an act that involves our entire being (body, soul, mind, and spirit) as we present ourselves to the Almighty.

Saturday morning worship in the synagogue is approximately two hours long. This may seem like a long time to some but it should be noted here that the Sabbath morning worship in the synagogue is very simple, straightforward, and prearranged. The synagogue is usually within walking distance from one's home, and the psalms to be read and the prayers to be prayed are generally dictated by the prayer book and seasons of the year. There is not a lot of preparation that goes into the Jewish worship service other than having read the Torah portion beforehand and the rabbi's giving a short homily concerning an aspect of the portion. The walk to and from the synagogue is often relaxing and provides an opportunity to talk with others. Therefore, outside of the two hours at the synagogue there is very little to be done in order to participate in the Saturday morning worship time.

The Second Meal

Religious Jews typically come home after their time at the synagogue in the morning and enjoy the second meal of the Sabbath. This meal usually begins around noon. Since religious Jews avoid doing any sort of work on the Sabbath, they have already prepared this meal. It simply needs to be served and eaten. This is the first meal eaten during the day of the Sabbath, since religious Jews generally do not eat breakfast before going to the synagogue.

The second meal is filled with songs and blessings similar to the first meal on Friday evening including the *zemirot* (poems/songs) about the Sabbath. The *kiddush* (the blessing over the wine) is prayed in a similar fashion as on Friday evening. In fact, the actual blessings over the wine, after the washing of the hands, and over the bread are exactly the same. Since the second meal mirrors the first meal in most respects, it is not necessary to repeat all of the activities of the meal. The main difference between the first meal and the second meal is that the familial blessings and songs preceding the first meal are not recited or sung preceding the second meal.

It should be noted that nothing is eaten before the *kiddush* (the blessing over the wine) is performed. As mentioned earlier, the blessing over the wine is the initial sanctifying act that separates the meal on the Sabbath as special from all the other meals eaten during the week. Therefore, at the beginning of this meal on Saturday the blessing is said over the wine and this is followed by the washing of hands and the blessing over the bread. Once the blessing over the bread is recited and everyone takes a bite, everyone is free to eat and drink at leisure.

During this second meal of the Sabbath, as at the first meal, there is generally a discussion of the Torah portion. Someone may share for several minutes about something that they learned from the Torah portion, or different people around the table may simply be given the opportunity to share their thoughts. Either way, there is generally a focus on spiritual things during some part of this meal so as not to become overly focused on the physical meal alone. After the meal has been eaten the special blessing for the food, the "Birkat Hamazon," is said to give thanks to God.

The second meal, like the first, is to be a meal where there is plenty of food mixed with a lot of social interaction. A sample schedule has been included at the end of this chapter to help provide structure for the second meal.

Practical Applications

How will you choose to spend your Sabbath morning?

It may be that your family will want to have a leisurely morning. It might be best for your family not to have an organized program for Saturday morning. This should be permitted one day per week. It is nice not to have to go somewhere, be somewhere, or do something one day a week. The Sabbath is supposed to be about rest so one need not feel guilty.

On the other hand, your family may choose to spend time in an organized worship setting like a synagogue or a church. If so, it is important to keep focused and devote your entire being: body, soul, mind, and spirit to an encounter with the Almighty. Even if those around you are getting caught up in routine and seem distracted, I would encourage you to make the most of the situation and learn something new. Ask God to show you something new about Himself when you go to worship. Before you go to your place of worship, try to go with a prepared mind. As a Christian, there are things you can do to prepare yourself. Most churches I attended as a child had pastors who taught on different subjects or from different parts of the Bible for weeks on end. If possible, prepare yourself ahead of time by reading from the text that will be taught in order to make the most of the worship time.

If you choose to have a spiritual time with your family at home instead of going to a church, then I would recommend that the father of the home take the lead in the worship time and in delegating any responsibilities to others in the family. If he is unable to lead the family in the worship time someone else should be assigned this responsibility. I would also encourage all those involved to read the selected Scripture or Torah portion sometime during the week. Think about some of the lessons to be learned from it or ask questions that may be discussed as a family. The worship time on the Sabbath does not need to be elaborate. It need not require a great deal of preparation on the Sabbath day itself. It should be a simple worship time in which all who attend feel included and refreshed spiritually.

The Sabbath is meant to be a day that is fulfilling and rejuvenating in all aspects: physically, emotionally, and spiritually. Physically there should be plenty of rest and food. Enjoying the second meal together as a family, with discussion throughout, will continue to build family relationships and will help meet both physical and emotional needs. In addition, it is worthwhile to incorporate something to nourish your spirit. If your family incorporates a spiritual worship time into your lives during the week, then bring it into your Sabbath day of rest by talking about it together as a family. If an organized worship time is not part of your week, I would encourage you to try to make it a part of your Sabbath day. It is best to avoid traveling long distances and participate in local worship, if possible. This will help keep your Sabbath day more restful, especially for the driver. Whether your worship time is at home or at a local place of worship, do your best to keep the family together and involved in God-centered rest!

New Testament Connections

1. As mentioned in the previous chapter, it is easy to tie the Torah portion of the week to Scriptures in the New Testament. It is recommended that someone from the family be responsible to study the Torah portion and make connections to the New Testament. In addition to the Torah portion there are the Psalms and other Scriptures that are read weekly and can be connected to the New Testament as well. Several examples of this can be found below.

2. The Akeidah (which is translated as "the binding" i.e. of Isaac) from Genesis 22 is a powerful story to think and talk about. Abraham is given the promise of having a son in his old age. The promise comes true and then a few years later God asks Abraham to take his own son's life by tying him up and putting him upon the altar as a sacrifice. The New Testament speaks of Abraham over and over. One section of the New Testament that specifically relates to this account of Abraham being tested by God is found in the book of Hebrews:

> *By faith Abraham, when he was tested, offered up Isaac; and he who had received the promises was offering up his only begotten son; it was he to whom it was said, 'IN ISAAC YOUR DESCENDANTS SHALL BE CALLED.' He considered that God is able to raise men even from the dead; from which he also received him back as a type (11:17-19).*

This account of Abraham being tested to the limit reminds us of how much we need to trust God when we go through the deep valleys of life. It also teaches us that God can do the impossible. God may call on us to do things that seem impossible, but we need to follow Him with complete devotion as Abraham did and trust Him for the outcome.

3. The "Shema" and the corresponding section about loving God are actually quoted by Jesus in the New Testament. The Shema comes from Deuteronomy 6:

Hear, O Israel! The LORD is our God, the LORD is one! And you shall love the LORD your God with all your heart and with all your soul and with all your might. (6:4-6)

Jesus quotes these exact verses from the Torah in a discussion with someone recorded in the New Testament:

And one of the scribes came and heard them arguing, and recognizing that He had answered them well, asked Him, 'What commandment is the foremost of all?'
Jesus answered:
The foremost is, 'Hear, O Israel! The LORD OUR GOD IS ONE LORD: AND YOU SHALL LOVE THE LORD YOUR GOD WITH ALL YOUR HEART, AND WITH ALL YOUR SOUL, AND WITH ALL YOUR MIND, AND WITH ALL YOUR STRENGTH.' The second is this, 'YOU SHALL LOVE YOUR NEIGHBOR AS YOURSELF.' There is no other commandment greater than these.' (Mark 12:28-31)

In His response, Jesus takes that which is familiar to all Jews and adds this extra part (the second commandment) about loving your neighbor. This is another quote from the

Torah, found in Leviticus 19:18. The combining of these two commandments was not mere coincidence. There is a textual reason evident in the Hebrew language that makes it easy to bring these commands into a unifying statement.

As you study the different aspects of the Sabbath service you will find many connections in the New Testament.

The Second Meal

(A sample schedule)

Saturday Morning

- **Morning worship**
- ***Kiddush* (the blessing over the wine)**
- **First course: fresh fruit**
- **A Psalm is read or a song is sung together**
- **Washing of hands**
- **Second course: blessing over the bread**
    - Different types of salads
    - Olives & pickles
    - A variety of sauces (such as humus) for the bread
- **A short discussion about the Torah portion**
- **The main course**
    - Meat with vegetables
    - or Quiche with different cheeses
- **Giving thanks after the meal**

Chapter 9

The Heart of the Sabbath: REST

There is an appointed time for everything.
And there is a time for every event under
heaven
Ecclesiastes 3:1

The Sabbath was instituted so that man could rest. After the second meal (lunch/brunch) on Saturday, some take a nap, others read, and some go for a walk. There seem to be unlimited possibilities as to how one may spend free time on the Sabbath. Or are there?

Religious Jews adhere to clear guidelines during the Sabbath. There are many rules along with some gray areas and there may be different rules according to the rabbi one follows. Bearing this in mind, there is an accepted list of thirty nine creative activities that have been compiled by the rabbis defining activities that should be refrained from on the Sabbath. For the sake of simplicity, I have summed up this list and combined them with everyday activities to present *"The Five Do's and Don'ts for the Sabbath."* These are "guidelines" that I have seen generally practiced by religious Jews and not an exhaustive summary of the actual list. It is simply one means to familiarize the reader with an example of how a religious Jewish person practices the Sabbath.

Jewish Tradition

Five things a religious Jew will DO on the Sabbath:

1. Make *kiddush* (say the blessings or at least hear them) before the two main meals: Friday evening and Saturday lunch
2. Eat and drink well
3. Spend time with family, friends, and/or neighbors
4. Spend time at the synagogue and pray
5. Read and discuss the Torah portion of the week

Five things a religious Jew will AVOID DOING on the Sabbath:

1. Work
2. Carry or spend money.
3. Light a fire, use electricity, or use electronics
4. Play a musical instrument
5. Travel using a motorized vehicle or walk beyond a certain distance.

There are obvious limitations concerning what a Jew who is trying to live a "Torah observant life" can and cannot do. The challenge regarding this subject is that there is generally more focus on what one ***cannot*** do in religious circles than on what one ***can*** do. The above is a basic outline. I will not go into more detail surrounding this but simply wanted to provide a glimpse into the day of rest lived out by a religious Jewish community.

Since this chapter is devoted to ideas regarding how to spend a day resting, I will focus on ideas related to spending leisure time. As a family, you may decide not to plan anything specific during your free time on Saturday afternoon. The suggestions given in this chapter are ideas for those who want to keep everyone involved and occupied during the Sabbath.

Practical Applications

Planned Rest

Most of us are not used to scheduling our free time, especially a restful day within community. There may be those who schedule a nap from time to time, and we are great at scheduling a tennis match, a basketball game, or coffee with a friend at Starbucks, but the majority of us do not plan a whole day to simply enjoy and rest.

If one identifies with the religious community, it may be suitable to go to a place of worship at some point during the Sabbath. A focused time of worship that is surrounded by quiet and rest in one's life can be the closest one can come to heaven on earth, a sort of oasis in the desert. Worship, however, is not usually an all day event. The question arises as to how one fills those remaining eight to ten hours.

Each person must be convinced in their own mind concerning what the Bible says is right and proper to do on the Sabbath, a day of rest. As a parent, you may have the extra responsibility and privilege to think this through with or for your children, thus providing a framework in which to function. As much as I think it is a beautiful thing to have family traditions and boundaries for the Sabbath, I also know that it can become a great source of tension between children and parents. There must be clear communication about why certain things are done and flexibility at times so as not to become overly rigid.

The creation of a Sabbath day for a family may take time to develop. The intertwining of rest with relationship is complex and it will require great care and wise planning to do this for a family. The key will be to keep it simple, keep it free from exhausting preparation, and to choose things that will restore and rejuvenate your family rather than deplete them of energy.

Some questions to consider:

- What activities does your family enjoy? In other words, what do you like to do together?
- Which activities would be beneficial to incorporate into your Sabbath day of rest as a family?
- What is it that you can do on the Sabbath that you cannot normally do during the other six days of the week? If you sit at a computer forty to sixty hours each week, you may need to spend the Sabbath with a little more activity. If you are a construction worker or a waitress at a restaurant and are on your feet all day, you will probably choose to rest and stay at home. A mother who stays at home with a young child or young children may prefer to get out of the house and not be confined to the four walls of the home. Or, she may enjoy some personal time while dad takes the children to the park.
- Consider the things you want to avoid doing during your Sabbath day, because you know it will distract your family from rest.
- Think about a weekly activity that you would like to see your family practice with a five to ten year focus. What do you want your family to experience during the Sabbath that will positively affect each one for the rest of their lives?

For many people, coming up with a workable plan for a Sabbath day will be fun and enjoyable. If you find yourself becoming focused on the details to the point that it becomes a chore, it may be advisable to stop and consider the long-range plan and the spiritual benefits. Remember that Jesus said that the Sabbath was made for man and not man for the Sabbath.

For Those Without Hobbies

There is a married couple that I have known for most of my life. I grew up with their children and they have seen me grow from a boy to who I am today. The husband has his own business. He enjoys working and does well at it. He gets things done and is a great people person. This couple is the same age as my parents. My father is retired and has been for about ten years. When I see this couple and we start talking, I ask the husband if he is thinking about retiring. He thinks for a second and then looks at me and says, "I think about it but what would I do if I stopped working? I enjoy working and I would be bored if I did not work." I then ask him, "Do you not have any hobbies?" He responds, "No!" I then suggest that he find some hobbies.

What do you do if you do not have any hobbies?

I have to admit that this is a difficult question for me to answer. I have so many things that I enjoy doing that if I never had another day of "work" in my life I would never be bored. Things like reading, playing guitar, playing tennis, skiing, hiking, camping, riding a bike, riding a motorcycle, and gardening are things I enjoy, just to name a few. Therefore, when I hear people tell me that they do not have any hobbies I think to myself, "How can that be? There are so many wonderful things in life to enjoy!"

As I think back on my own childhood I remember consciously choosing certain things to learn, to invest my time in, and to master. Riding motorcycles and fixing them was something that I simply did like breathing. I would be on a motorcycle every spare minute of the day if I was not fixing it or replacing parts to make it go faster or look better. Other hobbies such as playing tennis and skiing took more effort and discipline. When I began to play the guitar I believe I quit about ten times before I really started playing. It was not fun at first like hopping on a motorcycle. It took discipline to learn the chords and notes of a guitar and it was painful building calluses on my fingertips so that I could eventually play with ease and feel the joy of chords coming together.

These hobbies mentioned above I did by myself or with friends. Downhill skiing was something I originally did with friends but then it developed into a family activity. My sisters started skiing with friends and then my Dad learned as well so that we could ski as a family. He would organize trips for us and we would ski together. I have some wonderful memories of those times together.

Obviously, skiing is not generally something to do for a weekly Sabbath practice, unless you own a house in the mountains with some good skiing nearby. I only share this to relate how my family began to bond around a certain activity that literally took years, lots of hard work, and a financial investment to bring about an experience that we could all enjoy together. It is the same principle with the practice of the Sabbath. It generally is not something that will just happen. You must be intentional. Try different activities, learn from others, invest time and possibly money, and be creative. Below is a list of potential activities to incorporate into your family's day of rest.

Some positive suggestions for your day of rest:

- **Games:** Play a game together as a family. It could be a card game, a board game, or a mind game. The game could be educational in nature for families that teaches moral principles or tools for life. It could also just be a game that allows everyone to laugh a lot and have a good time with one another.
- **Sharing:** Talk about some highlights from the past week. Give everyone in your family a chance to share something positive that happened or perhaps something challenging. Giving children this weekly opportunity to share from their lives will give them something to anticipate and provide a good outlet with trusted people.
- **Discussion:** Have a family discussion about the Torah portion, a certain holiday that is coming up, or some other meaningful topic.
- **Sing:** Have a new song that is introduced each week. It could be a religious song, a folk song, or something fun.
- **Visit Others:** Neighbors, friends, or family.
- **Light Exercise:** Go for a walk together in a park, to the mountains, on a beach, or whatever is close by.
- **Absorb Nature:** Sit on the balcony, on the porch, or in the back yard and simply enjoy creation. Hopefully you live in such a place. If not, try to find a suitable location.

Suggestions for families with children:

- **Sports:** Play an outdoor game with the kids: kick ball, wiffle ball, Frisbee, etc…
- **Bicycling:** Bicycling as a family is a great way to spend time together and enjoy different scenery outdoors. It also builds team spirit as you wait for each other and help each other along the way. (If physical activity is part of your daily life as a family, bicycling on the Sabbath may not be restful for you.)

- **Story Time:** For parents of younger children, read a certain story that is only read on the Sabbath.
- **Drama:** For parents of school-age children, one of the parents or an older sibling could lead the children in putting on a short, weekly skit or drama. This could be taken from the Torah portion, another section of the Bible, or something topical. I have done this with different groups of children and have found that children generally enjoy acting and enthusiastically participate. However, they typically need guidance until a certain age. This will require a good deal of preparation for someone to think through the different roles and lines. Although, you could simply come up with a story and characters and give the children more freedom to ad-lib rather than having to create an entire play. Bible characters such as Noah, Abraham, Isaac, Jacob, Joseph, Esther, Ruth, and Daniel all provide great stories for kids to act out.
- **Focus on Nature:** Have a weekly nature walk on your Sabbath with a short lesson about nature. Children enjoy learning and exploring the outdoors. Take this opportunity to teach them about trees, flowers, wildlife, or whatever else may be fitting for your situation.
- **Picnic/swimming:** Spend the day or part of the day at a nearby lake or at the beach. Go swimming if the weather is nice. Bring food with you and have a picnic by the water.
- **Youth Activities:** Something common in modern Orthodox Jewish circles is something called Bnei Akiva, a Jewish youth movement. There are activities (songs, games, etc…) organized for young people Friday evening and Saturday afternoon after the main meal times. Having some sort of organized youth activities for the young people can enable them to enjoy the Sabbath into their

adult years. (Note that these activities are arranged after the family meal times and do not conflict with the family times.)

Suggestions for communities:

- **Athletics:** Younger communities will probably prefer to be more active. Play a sport together, go for a hike in the mountains, or go for a long bike ride. Spend the day boating, canoeing, surfing, or swimming at a lake or river. Go rollerblading or ice skating.
- **Make Music:** If there are several musicians in your community, spend a few hours playing some of your favorite songs together or make up new ones.
- **Games:** Play a board game, mind game, or cards.
- **The Arts:** For mature communities plan a trip to a museum, a play, an art exhibit, or a seasonal event: i.e. a fall festival.
- **Back to Nature:** If your community enjoys the outdoors, plan a few hours to pick a certain fruit that is in season: apples, blueberries, strawberries, etc…
  (The people that are part of your unique community will help determine the activities that you choose for your day of rest.)

Individual activities: Within a family/community there are also times of individual rest.

- **Read:** a book, a magazine, the Bible, etc…
- **Solitude:** Just rest, relax and enjoy the silence.
- **Play a musical instrument:** As long as it does not disturb others.
- **Listen to music**

As much as I want to give suggestions I also want to refrain from doing so, because I know that some of you will want to try each one and check it off week by week to say that you have done all of these. We are made to achieve and strive but we are also made (or rather commanded) to rest. To achieve and strive is generally what we do all week long, so please keep in mind that the primary command of the Sabbath is to rest and remember what God has already created and given to us. The ideas presented in this chapter are only suggestions to possibly include in your day of rest. Each family or community will have to make wise decisions about the essential components to include during a day of rest.

It may be difficult for some of us to rest. Note that in my short list of suggestions nothing requires the television, a DVD player, or anything of this nature. I enjoy watching a good movie now and then, but it is nice to set these things aside at least once a week and actively pursue time with others.

Cease striving and know that I am God... (Psalm 46:10).

This is one of my favorite verses from the Psalms. When life does not go as planned and it seems that I have lost all control, I reflect on this verse and enjoy releasing all of my fears and anxieties to God. As I reflect on the magnitude of God, I feel silly for thinking that somehow I was actually in control. This perspective helps as we begin to take our rest more seriously. God is in control and we simply need to be still. Ideally, it would be great to live in such a way that this verse is a reality 24/7. Until then, take one day a week and try to put this verse into practice. Be still! Set the things from work aside, think on God, and enjoy the people around you.

Reality Check: A look into my Sabbath

A typical Sabbath for me (depending on where I am in the world and who I am with) is a Sabbath type meal on Friday evening with a group of friends or a family. If there is a synagogue close by I try to attend the Friday evening service as well as the Saturday morning service, though I am not one who feels obligated to be there every week. On Saturdays, after the morning worship time and the second meal are finished, I typically do not have the day planned out. I may read a book, or part of one. I may listen to music or play the guitar. I may take a short walk outside if the weather is nice and enjoy some fresh air. I may spend the day with friends or family talking about life and enjoying relationships or I may just rest and take a two-hour nap.

There are also times when I am with a family or in community and our meal times last for three to four hours both on Friday evening and Saturday afternoon. When this is the case the only thing I want to do during the times in between is rest, sleep, and maybe read. Free time for families and individuals in a community during a day of rest is just as important as planned meals and planned worship. The key is to develop some sort of workable plan with enjoyable and life-giving activities as needed without wearing everyone out.

New Testament Connections

Jesus takes a unique approach to the concept of rest in His teaching. He invites people to come to Him in order to find rest. Jesus offers His followers a spiritual rest that seems to go beyond the week-to-week practice of a physical day of rest. In one of His famous talks around the Sea of Galilee Jesus spoke these words:

Come to Me, all who are weary and heavy-laden, and I will give you rest. Take My yoke upon you, and learn of Me, for I am gentle and humble in heart; and YOU SHALL FIND REST FOR YOUR SOULS. For My yoke is easy, and My load is light. (Matthew 11:28-30)

Rest is the goal of "Practicing the Sabbath" and it should include all areas of life: physical, emotional, mental, and spiritual.

Chapter 10

The Intent of the Sabbath: LIFE

Is it lawful on the Sabbath to do good
or to do harm, to save a life or to kill?
Mark 3:4

It may not be easy to determine the activities in which your family will participate during a Sabbath day of rest. In this book I have attempted to provide some general parameters and a few ideas that might be utilized in establishing a Sabbath day. However, your family will have to determine how best to observe the Sabbath according to the individual needs of each member. In this chapter, I would like to present another important element of the Sabbath day which should be given some attention. This important element is service to others.

Jewish Tradition

Service to Others

Areas of service come in many forms in different societies. A very important service in Israeli society is security. The nation of Israel is surrounded by hostile enemies that would like to see physical harm done to both the nation as a whole and to the individual people living within its borders. As a result of this, Israeli security (police, the military, and local security services) must always be on alert. There is no avoiding this. What, therefore, happens on the Sabbath? Does the entire security force simply clock out and return to their homes for a day of rest? Of course not! There is always a crew of men and women who are on duty during the Sabbath in Israel to ensure that those who are enjoying their day of rest can do so in peace.

There are also medical services that must be kept operating at all times. Hospitals, fire stations, ambulance services, medical-response teams, and elder-care must always keep some personnel working (or ready to work) during the Sabbath. These individuals sacrifice time with their families on the Sabbath so that they may serve the people of their community.

Practical Applications

The people working in the different sectors listed are required to serve others because it is their job. Perhaps you or someone you know are in a similar situation? One may be a doctor, nurse, policeman, fire fighter, or caretaker of a sick or elderly person. In these cases a day of rest may be limited to being on call during one's free days. Or it may be nearly impossible for one to truly have a complete day of rest because someone else is always dependent upon them. Those who find themselves in one of these situations will have added complications in practicing a Sabbath day of rest. I would recommend, however, that we all do our best to work with others in our communities (family, friends, and/or coworkers) to have alternate days of rest. We all need to rest to ensure optimal functioning and for spiritual and physical renewal.

Choosing to Serve Others

There is another aspect to service that is important for us to consider here, and that is choosing to serve others. Growing up in the Protestant-Christian world as I did, I can often recall this idea of service to others as being an important aspect of the teaching of Jesus. As was mentioned in Chapter Two of this book, Jesus focused on a deeper meaning of the Sabbath. He did not simply follow rules and guidelines but enjoyed the day and helped others along the way.

In the verse from the Gospel of Mark quoted at the head of this chapter, Jesus asked a question of those around Him who were opposed to Him healing on the Sabbath. A man sat in the synagogue with a withered hand and Jesus, having pity upon him, wanted to see this man restored and healed. Jesus then raised the question of what the "lawful" thing is to do on the Sabbath, "to do good or to do harm, to save a life or to kill?" Jesus then heals the man, answering His own question with an action. It was the Sabbath.

In another situation from the New Testament, it is recorded that Jesus healed a man who had some sort of illness which left him unable to walk. Jesus had asked the man if he wanted to get well. After the man responded, Jesus commanded him to "Arise, take up your pallet, and walk" (John 5:8). And he did! This event also took place on the Sabbath and some people were not too happy with Jesus doing these sorts of things on this special day. Jesus' response to them was, "My Father is working until now, and I Myself am working" (John 5:17). Jesus makes a very bold statement here about how God is His Father and declares boldly that He and the Father, God in heaven, are both "working," even on the Sabbath. These statements are difficult for religious Jews to even consider. I will only focus on what Jesus said regarding His working on the Sabbath. Again, in keeping with Jesus' teaching, I truly believe that Jesus was not canceling out the validity of the Sabbath or saying it was good for everyone to work on the Sabbath. However, He was emphasizing that it is good to show **kindness** and **mercy** on the Sabbath for the sake of helping someone in need. Showing mercy to others on the Sabbath and at other times is the true "work" of God and, therefore, it must be our work as well without regard to the day of the week.

Ways of Serving Others

There are different ways that we may serve others on our Sabbath day that can be very fulfilling and a true gift to others. One way to serve others is to practice hospitality. Invite another family, a couple, or a single person to join you and your family during your day or part of your day of rest. There may be some new neighbors in your area or a colleague and their family that could use some kindness. There are more than likely some children in your neighborhood that do not have a good family situation and they could use some time away from their own home environment. Inviting them to participate in the games you play with your own children or one of the other ways in which you spend time together on the Sabbath could be a great service to them. Consider showing hospitality on your Sabbath day.

Another way of serving others is to visit someone who is sick or elderly, whether a family member or not. Spending time with someone in this situation is a great gift, and bringing them food or some small gift can even further demonstrate that much thought went into the visit. If you do not know someone in need you could do something that I used to do with my youth group. We visited the local nursing home. The nursing home staff is generally more than willing to have visitors spend time with their residents because many residents do not have family to look after them. Consider taking an hour or so during your weekly day of rest to show kindness to those who are sick, lonely, or elderly. Along the same lines, you could visit someone you know who is in prison. We may not realize how important a visit is from someone, but it speaks more than ten thousand words or all the riches that one can accumulate.

During my college days some friends and I would take one day a month and volunteer with an inner-city, non-profit organization to help homeless people. We would make lunches for the homeless people and sometimes collect clothes. Then we would meet at a certain place where this organization worked and assist in distributing food and clothing to the homeless. It took a lot of effort but it was also very rewarding for my friends and me. We were all single, young, and had plenty of time on our hands so, depending on your family or community situation, something like this may or may not be appropriate.

Precautions!!!

As much as I believe that serving others during a Sabbath day is a beautiful idea, I also know that it can easily slip into a day of complete service without rest. As you are intentional about service to others, try to limit it to that which is appropriate for your family and your individual situation.

I have a good friend who is married with three children. Their family tries to keep a weekly day of rest together. Their children are all school-age and therefore have many friends in the neighborhood. My friend and his wife will include some of the neighborhood children in their family activities during their Sabbath, but they also try to limit how much time these neighborhood children spend with their family during their day of rest. Their children play with the neighborhood children almost every day, so my friend and his wife try to make their Sabbath day different by limiting the flow of children into their home. I believe this is a wise choice which allows this couple to genuinely have some personal time with their own children on their Sabbath day.

As this chapter comes to a close I want to encourage you to consider how you and your family will incorporate service into your Sabbath day. This suggestion is by no means a rule you must keep. It is completely permissible to choose not to include some type of service on your Sabbath, particularly if you are already involved in a service profession. If you do choose to include some type of service to others, please carefully consider how to do it and set proper boundaries to protect your own family.

Despite all of my different suggestions mentioned in this chapter, I personally believe it is wise not to do any unnecessary traveling on the Sabbath. The more you are able to serve others in your own home the better you will be able to protect your own Sabbath day of rest. There may be times when your duty as a security officer, a medical professional, or a caretaker will force you to serve others outside of your home. There may be other times that you choose to serve others. Either way, I strongly encourage you to do all you can to plan your Sabbath day well. The key to a successful Sabbath will be proper preparation. This is the focus of the next chapter.

New Testament Connections

There are several New Testament verses that are applicable when thinking about service to others. The verses listed below are not linked to the Sabbath but they do depict the heart of God.

1. Hebrews 13:3

   Remember the prisoners, as though in prison with them, and those who are ill-treated, since you yourselves also are in the body.

This verse from the letter to the Hebrews is fairly straightforward with a reminder to remember those who are in prison and those who are being mistreated in some way. In the comfort of our home with family and friends, we need to be mindful of those in other situations and take action when we are able and when it seems appropriate.

2. Matthew 25:35-36 (the words of Jesus)

> *For I was hungry, and you gave Me something to eat; I was thirsty, and you gave Me drink; I was a stranger, and you invited Me in; naked, and you clothed Me; I was sick, and you visited Me; I was in prison and you came to visit Me.*

Jesus was explaining a parable to His followers about the "Kingdom of Heaven" and how different ones will be rewarded on judgment day. Jesus told this gripping parable to explain to His followers that in serving others they are in fact serving Him.

Chapter 11

The Key to a Successful Sabbath: Preparation

See, the LORD has given you the sabbath;
therefore He gives you bread for two days
on the sixth day.
Exodus 16:29

One Friday while in Israel, I boarded the 9:30 am bus to the area of the University library. When I got on, I asked the bus driver what time the last bus would be returning to the area. The bus driver answered me but I did not fully hear him so I repeated it back to him to make sure I had heard him correctly. "Did you say 1:30 pm?", I asked. He thought I was questioning the validity of his answer as he looked at me and said sternly, "*Hayom, Yom Shishi*!" meaning "Today is the sixth day!" The sixth day in Israel is Friday, the second to last day of the week. Everyone in Israel knows that everything is different on Friday, the day before the Sabbath.

I knew exactly what he meant. Friday in Israel is preparation day for the Sabbath. On Fridays in the early afternoon, everything begins to close and people make their way home to prepare. The buses and trains stop running and the storeowners begin locking their doors. In the majority of places in Israel there is no escaping this reality. The Sabbath is an intrinsic part of Israeli culture and whether one participates in the traditions or not, everyone needs to conclude their business before mid-afternoon on Friday.

Jewish Tradition

In the Jewish mind the week revolves around the Sabbath and all days lead up to it. The Sabbath is enjoyed and after the Sabbath concludes, the countdown begins to the next Sabbath. The week is filled with work yet the day of rest with family and friends is a delight and the highlight of the week. What needs to be done in order to prepare for this major, weekly event?

In a religious Jewish home the wife focuses most of her time and energy on things concerning the home and the children. As a result of this, much of the physical preparation falls on the woman of the home and possibly the children. Today, however, many men do what they can to help and men can often be seen doing last-minute shopping.

The Sabbath for religious Jews provides motivation to clean the house. On either Thursday or Friday the house cleaning begins. The floors are swept, carpets shaken or vacuumed, and the furniture dusted.

Another major chore in the preparation process is the purchase of the necessary food. Since stores are closed in many places in Israel from mid-afternoon Friday until Saturday night or Sunday morning, proper planning of meals and purchasing of food is essential. Meal preparation is necessary for at least two full days so food is purchased on Thursday or Friday morning at the latest. Since one never knows if God may bring a guest or guests to the home, extra food is always prepared with them in mind. One food item that is usually purchased last (unless it is homemade) is *challah* bread in order to get the freshest possible loaves.

With the house cleaned and the food bought, the food preparations commence. Since religious Jews avoid working on the Sabbath, food is prepared before the Sabbath begins. Between Thursday and Friday meals are cooked for at least the upcoming day and a half. Typically, there are three main meals that are prepared for the Sabbath:

1. The first meal on Erev Shabbat (the Friday evening meal)
2. The second meal (eaten on Saturday around lunch time)
3. The third meal (eaten at the end of the day on Saturday)

Rather than try to make three totally separate meals most families make a few different main dishes, several types of salads, some type of soup, and several desserts. All are placed at each meal and everyone has a small amount of each so that the food stretches from Friday night to Saturday night without having to constantly create a new meal. As many of you know, planning meals for a family can be quite demanding and needs to be carefully thought through.

Once this has all been completed, the details of organizing the home are worked out. The dinner table is set with candles placed on it (or candles are placed somewhere else in the room) and all the necessary utensils, plates, bowls and glasses are arranged as needed. Religious Jews will sometimes use plastic bowls, plates, eating utensils, and other disposable items in order to make life simpler for everyone. In this way there are no dirty dishes to clean! All necessary household chores are taken care of so that nothing has to be done on the Sabbath. The laundry is washed and folded, beds are made, and everything is in its place.

Since the Sabbath is regarded as unique and festive as compared to the other days of the week, most people try to make an extra effort to be bathed and groomed before the Sabbath begins. Religious Jews do not bathe on the Sabbath so this is done sometime before Friday evening. Religious Jews will traditionally dress in special clothing on both Friday evening and Saturday. A man will wear his favorite shirt and trousers, and a woman her favorite dress. This is another way of signifying that this is a special day.

Ultra-religious men (Orthodox or *Haredi* Jews) generally have a certain type of outfit for the Sabbath: a special suit, robe, hat, and shoes. Color is usually not important. The standard colors for the more religious are simply black (trousers) and white (shirt). There are many different reasons for this, one of them being that they desire to be more like God's Word (the Torah) and less like the world around them. They also desire uniformity so that there is no difference between the rich and the poor.

Since religious Jews will not touch electrical appliances or anything electric during the Sabbath, many preparations are made in order not to turn on a lamp or oven. Lights are left on during this time in general areas: the kitchen, the bathroom, and dining room. The lights are purposely left off in the bedrooms and any other areas that would hinder sleeping at night. During the summer the air-conditioner may be left on so as to provide a comfortable environment, or during the winter the heater is set for a suitable temperature for the next twenty four hours.

Religious Jews typically use large, flat electric heating elements (called 'hot plates') in the kitchen that are set on low temperatures and left on for the duration of the Sabbath. Pots or dishes may be placed on these heating devices to heat food. Dishes are generally placed on these heaters an hour or two in advance. This eliminates actually turning switches on or off. Large electric hot water kettles are also filled and left on for the twenty four hours of the Sabbath so that hot water is available for tea and coffee.

The husband or father of the home is usually responsible for saying the blessings, guiding the Sabbath prayers and songs during the meals, and sharing something meaningful relating to the Torah portion. In preparation for this he will have studied the Torah portion of the week. In this way, he will be able to share significant insights during the times of spiritual focus.

With all this preparation, it may now be more clearly understood how the whole week revolves around this special day. There are many things to consider with regard to preparation for the Sabbath.

Practical Applications

The preparation aspect of the Sabbath is foundational with regard to having a pleasant day of rest. A successful Sabbath day is dependent upon the preparations for it throughout the week.

Since no two situations look alike, it is challenging to give input regarding the application of the ideas mentioned in this chapter. The key element in this regard is to work as a family in order to make the proper preparations that are needed for your day of rest. No one person should ever have to bear the burden of all that a Sabbath day requires.

Cleaning & Organizing the Home

The cleaning and organizing of the home as a family can easily be divided among the children and parents as seems fit. There needs to be clear communication with regard to who is responsible for what, including deadlines with a specific time on a particular day. This will help bring accountability. For friends that live together in community the same principle can obviously be applied. For the person living alone there is not much choice but to do the cleaning by oneself; although, if one has good friends, perhaps they would be willing to come over and help in this area.

Food Shopping

Depending on your family or community situation, the food shopping may be done by one person or shared by all who are willing. Most importantly, have a clear menu in mind for the day of rest so that adequate food is bought and prepared. For those in the non-traditional setting of community, it is wise to ask everyone to bring something so as to share the work and take some of the burden away from the host. Drinks, desserts, and salads are easily purchased or made and brought to the host's home.

Food Preparation

Preparing the food for the Sabbath is similar to how many people in America prepare for a certain holiday like Thanksgiving. So much food is made that it takes a few days to finish it. This is the same mindset regarding the Sabbath. One should not have one meal in mind but three or more.

Cooking may be one of the most time-consuming aspects of the preparation. For those who enjoy cooking, this will be a delight and for those who struggle with working in the kitchen, there are several ways to lighten the load. Preparing some sort of stew, chili, or casserole for a main dish is a wonderful way to combine meat and vegetables and cut down on making several different side dishes.

As with the purchase of the food, if one is single or living in community, others may contribute by preparing a dish of their own to share. I remember a time I was invited to a family's home to share a Sabbath meal with them on a Friday evening. Along with me another family was invited as well. The guest family brought several dishes of food so there was plenty of food for all.

Another option that will help to minimize the work involved in food preparation is to buy prepared food. This has been a growing trend in the United States where most supermarkets have cold and hot prepared foods readily available. It may be a bit more expensive and lacking that homemade touch but it is a very viable alternative, especially if one simply does not have the time to do all the shopping and cooking.

Personal Hygiene

This is something more personal that I will not say too much about. It is obviously a good idea to appear well groomed and present oneself in a respectable manner. Therefore, before the Sabbath begins, do whatever is necessary in regard to personal hygiene to enjoy your day of rest more fully.

Mechanical Preparations

If one is trying to keep a more traditional Sabbath this subject is obviously very important. One may replicate what is being done by the religious Jews as far as leaving lights on in certain rooms and off in others. For those who do not want to follow the religious ways but still want to enjoy their day of rest with minimal distractions, it is best to adopt some of these practices as well. If one has a family or a larger community, the use of the large, commercial size electric hot water heater for tea and coffee can be very practical.

With our technological world it is becoming increasingly easy to program the central air conditioner or heating system for a week at a time and not have to worry about the temperature in the home. Lights can also be programmed along with almost any electrical items one may need to use.

The important thing is not to copy the Jewish ways but to make the Sabbath less stressful and more relaxing. What are some things that can be done to simplify and make your Sabbath more restful? What are some things that you really want to avoid doing on the Sabbath? Try to think of creative ways to handle each situation. Discuss your situations and ideas with others and I am sure that there will be a plethora of creative ideas to enable you to enjoy your Sabbath more fully.

The Mitzvah of Entertaining the Guest

The mitzvah ("the command" or "good deed") of entertaining guests must always be kept in mind. To entertain guests, especially on the Sabbath, is considered a great honor for the host or hostess in Judaism.

I was reminded of this once when I was sharing the Sabbath with some friends. I was in Jerusalem and I was to be a guest in the home of a friend, Jonathan, who regularly hosts people in his home for the Sabbath. I had been to Jonathan's home several times and each time there had been a unique group of people there along with his family. He lives in a secluded area in Jerusalem so he generally meets his guests at a certain location in the city and then he walks them to his home.

In times past when I have gone to Jonathan's home there have been between ten to fifteen people sitting around the long table situated in the center of his dining room. He believes in the philosophy "the more the merrier;" this time, however, it was the merriest of them all. As we began to walk to his home many in the group began to discuss if there was really going to be enough room for everyone to be seated and enjoy the evening meal. He kept reassuring us all that there would be plenty of space and plenty of food.

We arrived at his home and began filling his dining room. As we began to sit down at the table it became obvious that there were not going to be enough seats. He kept reassuring everyone that he would work it out. He got out a folding table and set it up with eight or ten more chairs and, though the room was full, everyone had a seat and there was plenty of food for everyone.

Before our very eyes Jonathan lived out this principle that the guest is to be honored. He did not want anyone to feel excluded or unwelcome. He did not begin to count people when he first met us to determine if there were too many, because he knew that this would make some in the group feel uncomfortable. He simply took as many people as came that day and welcomed us all into his home. He made a comfortable place for everyone and fed all thirty five of us while leading us through an evening of prayers, songs, stories, and laughter. Jonathan understands the mitzvah of entertaining the guest. He understands that the Sabbath is not simply a time to be used for self. He understands that the day is a gift from God to be used for rest but also a gift to be used to bless others.

I hope this story serves as an example of how we should view our Sabbath. I am not saying that you need to have an open house every Friday night in your home with as many guests as will come. Rather, I want to remind you that the Sabbath can be used as a time to show hospitality to others.

Whenever I have Sabbath meals at my home, I generally receive phone calls a day or two before from friends whom I have invited. They usually call to tell me that they will be attending, and ask if they can bring a friend or two. Sometimes I get frustrated at situations like this because I want to have everything under control and I always want there to be plenty of food. I have learned, however, that there is always enough food no matter how many people God brings to my table.

**Let us remember
to practice hospitality by honoring guests
during our Sabbath rest!**

Overnight Lodging

Since a family generally lives in one home together I did not mention the topic of lodging in the preparation for the Sabbath, but as we talk about entertaining guests this becomes an issue. Religious Jews will typically not drive on the Sabbath and will only walk a specified distance from their home or outside of the boundaries of their community/city. The standard limit for a Sabbath walk is 2000 cubits (about 3000 feet or a little more than a half a mile). If anyone comes to visit for the Sabbath and they live beyond the prescribed limit, it is assumed that they will stay the night and enjoy the entire Sabbath day with the family they are visiting. If people are living in the same area, within the prescribed distance, then it is not necessary to provide lodging for the guest(s). Providing lodging for guests is another consideration when preparing for a Sabbath celebration.

The Spiritual Dimension

For the family or community celebrating the Sabbath together, it is beneficial to have a spiritual focus during the time together since the day is a gift from God to us. It is best to designate someone to take the lead in this area or to have one person lead at each meal throughout the twenty four hour period. To keep individuals from having to prepare something on the Sabbath day itself, it is best to delegate the responsibility of bringing a devotion or teaching a few days beforehand.

For those who wish to follow the Hebrew calendar, discussing the Torah portion (see Supplement A) of the week is always enlightening. In order to follow the Jewish calendar with regard to the Torah portion, one can easily find information on the internet as to the section of the Torah for a particular week. Simply do a search on "Torah portion" or obtain a schedule from a local synagogue. Regarding the Torah portion, one option is to have an individual who is responsible for summarizing the Torah portion (or whatever Scripture you choose) and then go around and have each person share their thoughts on how it can be applied to real life. I have found this practice very helpful and insightful because we all see things from different perspectives.

Being well prepared in the area of spiritual input is wise. Though talking about things "off the cuff" may be pleasant, the conversation may go in many different directions and the focus of the spiritual dimension may easily turn to topics that may be less edifying.

The Children

In a family where children are participating, keeping the children involved in all areas is important. Let them have a say about the flow of the Sabbath. Allow them to pick a song and sing it if they are able or share what they think about the Scripture that has been taught. When they are mature enough, give them opportunity to lead the spiritual time. It is easy to give children small tasks like setting or cleaning the table. The more they help with buying the food, making a salad, making cookies, giving their thoughts about the Scripture, singing a song, planning an activity and so forth, the more they will feel connected to the whole concept of the Sabbath.

Reality Check: Preparation

I remember one time when I was invited to a family's home to spend the Sabbath with them. I was supposed to be there by 5pm on a Friday evening. In order to get myself ready and be on time, my preparations had to start on Thursday evening. After work on Thursday, I stopped at the grocery store to buy a bottle of wine to bring with me to their home. I took care of some things at home on Friday morning. I did laundry, cleaned my house, packed for the weekend, and got ready to go. I had to leave my home by about 1 pm because the last bus left from my neighborhood at that time. Since I had a couple of extra hours in the afternoon before I needed to be at their home, I visited some friends that lived nearby. Then I made my way to the family's home to join them for the Sabbath meal and arrived around 5 pm.

Even though I was not hosting an evening meal at my house, my preparations began on Thursday evening and continued throughout Friday morning and led up to the beginning of the Sabbath, Friday evening. I needed to take care of as much as possible so that I could truly rest and enjoy my time with this family. It was not simply a matter of getting to a certain place at a certain hour, but more of preparing myself to enter into a day of rest and being ready for the week ahead.

As a single person it takes focus to keep a weekly Sabbath. As a family it will take so much more. "Practicing the Sabbath" is not simply something nice to do once in a while. It is a way of life and it will take a lot of work, organization, and creativity. Take your time and prepare well! It will be worth it in the end.

New Testament Connections

Let love of the brethren continue. Do not neglect to show hospitality to strangers, for by this some have entertained angels without knowing it. (Hebrews 13:1-2)

Keeping the guest in mind is always a good rule of thumb!

The Sabbath:
A Typical Week at a Glance

- **Sunday – Friday:**
  - Study of the Torah portion in spare time
- **Thursday – Friday:**
  - Food is bought and prepared
  - The home is cleaned and organized
- **Friday Morning:**
  - The Sabbath table is set
  - Final preparations are made
- **Friday Afternoon:**
  - Last-minute details are attended to
  - Some people take a nap
  - Sometime during late afternoon personal hygiene is taken care of.
- **Friday Evening:**
  - Candles are lit before sunset
  - Men (and women & children if they wish) make their way to the synagogue
  - Everyone returns home for the evening meal (the First Meal) and activities
- **Saturday Morning:**
  - Worship time at the synagogue
- **Saturday About Noon:**
  - The Second Meal: Brunch
- **Saturday Afternoon:**
  - Rest or Sabbath day activities
- **Saturday Evening: (before sunset)**
  - The Third Meal
- **Saturday Evening: (after sunset)**
  - *Havdalah* – Greeting the new week

Chapter 12

The Conclusion of the Sabbath: Blessing the New Week

The conclusion, when all has been heard, is:
fear God and keep His commandments,
because this applies to every person.
For God will bring every act to judgment,
everything which is hidden, whether it is good or evil.
Ecclesiastes 12:13-14

As the Sabbath comes to an end for religious Jews there is a special ceremony called "*Havdalah*" which marks the end of this day and ushers in the beginning of the new week. This traditional ceremony takes place either in the synagogue or in the home and is one of the shortest ceremonies during the entire Sabbath celebration. Perhaps the reason for this is that it contains a little sadness in saying goodbye to this day of rest.

Jewish Tradition

To prepare for the close of the Sabbath, religious Jews typically eat their third meal approximately an hour before the sun sets, just prior to the *Havdalah* ceremony. The "third meal" is the final meal eaten during the Sabbath day. Compared to the first two meals, this final meal is very simple and short, lasting less then an hour. All of the formalities are dropped and it is a light meal in which the participants reflect upon the day of rest.

The Conclusion of the Sabbath - Three Stars!

The rabbis have been pondering how to fix the exact time for the conclusion of the Sabbath over the centuries and they have established their criteria for the transition from one day to another. They have determined that a day officially ends and another begins when one is able to see three stars in the sky! If only one star is seen, it could be an airplane or some other strange light, therefore, there needs to be the witness of three. The important element here is not "star counting" per se, rather, it is establishing a clear guide for all to follow to provide an exit from this glorious time of rest.

The Concluding Ceremony – "*Havdalah*"

Three main elements are part of the *Havdalah* ceremony: a special braided candle with several wicks (typically three), a cup of wine, and a special fragrance from a spice or herb (for example cloves, rosemary, or mint leaves). The candle is lit and it is either held by someone or placed in a holder and the glass of wine is filled to the top of the cup.

As I think about *Havdalah*, the word "Salvation" comes to mind because this is a central theme in the first blessing prayed during this ceremony. In this blessing the word "salvation" or some form of it is used six times. The blessing translated from the Hebrew is as follows:

Behold, God is my salvation, I will trust and not be afraid;
For the LORD GOD is my strength and song,
And He has become my salvation.

You shall draw water with joy
from the wells of salvation.
Salvation belongs to the LORD;
Thy blessing be upon Thy people!
Selah.
The LORD of hosts is with us;
The God of Jacob is our stronghold.
Selah.
O LORD of hosts,
How blessed is the man who trusts in Thee!
Save, O LORD;
May the King answer us in the day we call.
For the Jews there was light and gladness and joy and honor.
(Yes, may it be for us!)
I shall lift up the cup of salvation, And call upon the name of the LORD.

This blessing is actually a compilation of several different verses from the Bible: Isaiah 12:2-3; Psalms 3:8, 46:11, 84:12, 20:9, 116:13; and Esther 8:16. Note that the phrase in the second to last line of the above verses is not taken from the Bible but is said by all in the synagogue as a statement of agreement.

The repetitious use of the word *salvation* in this blessing is a continual reminder of the way in which God helps His people and how we must constantly depend on Him. As a religious Jew transitions from the Sabbath to the normal work week with all of the demands inherent in it, he or she needs to remember that God is the one in control and He alone is the source of one's help and salvation.

The blessing above is then followed by several short blessings. There is no discussion about these blessings and from start to finish the whole ceremony is over within a couple of minutes.

Immediately following the blessing above comes the traditional blessing over a full cup of wine:

Blessed are You, O Lord our God, King of the universe,
Creator of the fruit of the vine.

The wine signifies sanctification just as it did at the beginning of the Sabbath, though the wine is not drunk at this point. The glass is simply raised so the blessing may be recited. As discussed previously, wine is generally used to set someone or something apart. Here it signifies the end of the Sabbath and the beginning of the new week.

After the blessing of the wine another blessing is said over a sweet smelling spice:

Blessed are You, O Lord our God, King of the universe,
Creator of various kinds of spices.

After this blessing, each person inhales the aroma of the very fragrant spice. The purpose of the strong scent is to remind those who have just celebrated the Sabbath to remember it throughout the week ahead. As the fragrance is pleasant to one's senses so is the memory of the Sabbath.

Another blessing is then said in conjunction with the lit candle:

Blessed are You, O Lord our God, King of the universe,
Creator of the lights of the fire.

After this blessing those who hear it typically allow the light of the fire from the candle to reflect in their fingernails. This is another way to physically take in the experience of the Sabbath and its transition.

Finally, there is one last blessing:

Blessed are You, O Lord our God, King of the universe,
Who distinguishes between sacred and secular,
between light and darkness,
between Israel and the other nations,
between the seventh day and the six days of acting.
Blessed are You, O Lord,
Who distinguishes between sacred and secular.

After this final blessing, the person who has been reading drinks the cup of wine and extinguishes the candle by placing it in the spilled wine.

This last blessing is a good summary statement for anyone who is trying to describe the obvious distinctions in this world. No matter how one views Judaism, the truth is that God did create a division between secular and sacred, God did separate the light from the darkness when He created the world, and God did choose Israel from the other nations of the earth based on His promises to Abraham, Isaac, and Jacob. Finally, God did create the Sabbath separating it from the other days of the week.

This being said, I do not promote separating parts of our lives that fit into religion ("the sacred") and the remainder into the other parts of life ("the secular"). All of life is sacred to God and all that we do should be honoring to Him whether on the Sabbath or any other day of the week. However, there is a true principle of recognizing that there is a time and place for everything, including a day of rest.

In reference to Israel being set apart from other nations, in the final blessing above, it must be understood in the context of the Bible as a whole so as to not create an "air of superiority." God did not choose the Jewish people (the descendants of

Abraham, Isaac, and Jacob) because they were better or more numerous than other people. On the contrary, God Himself chose to love Israel and He desired to keep the covenant He made with Abraham, Isaac, and Jacob (Deuteronomy 7:6-8). One of God's purposes in choosing Israel (the Jewish people) was to be a light to the nations.

God desires people of every race, tongue, and nation to acknowledge His sovereignty and to obey Him. Acknowledging that God has chosen a specific nation in this world to represent His ways on earth does not elevate them as better than others. Instead, it bestows greater responsibility upon them. Religious Jewish people seek to obey God through honoring the Sabbath and by doing so, they remind the world around them of God's majesty and greatness in creating the world. Remembering God's sovereign hand in this world and recognizing that God has given us divine principles and a set order to follow is a paradigm shift that many in this world have yet to make.

At the conclusion of the *Havdalah* ceremony it is customary to say "*Shavua Tov*" to those you greet. "*Shavua Tov*" means "Have a good week" as we say in English; however, it carries with it a greater meaning. Just as "*Shabbat Shalom*" is declared at the beginning of the Sabbath, "*Shavua Tov*" is said to usher in the work week. "May you have a good week!" This is similar to what many people say around the world on New Years Day every year: "Happy New Year!" There are many blessings and expressions of good will that go along with this. For example, we may say, "May you and your family have a healthy and happy New Year!" We say these things to wish people well in the year to come. In the Jewish calendar this idea comes into focus every week, at the conclusion of the Sabbath, "*Shavua Tov*!" – "May your week be blessed and full of God's protection!"

Practical Applications

How will you choose to end your Sabbath? The activities mentioned in this chapter are not taken from the written Torah but they are traditions that have been developed and passed down by the Jewish people. These traditions mark one way to bring the Sabbath to a close and to do so at an official time. You may wish to adopt these practices as they are, or you may wish to create your own traditions concerning ending your Sabbath and entering back into the work week.

Some alternative options:

Option #1: Have a family meal at the close of the Sabbath whether it is in the morning, afternoon or evening. During the meal have a transition time, reflecting on the day of rest that has come to an end and discussing the events of the week ahead.

Option #2: If you end your Sabbath in the evening, have a meal before the day ends as the religious Jews do for their third meal. Then have a time of prayer after the sun sets to acknowledge that the Sabbath has ended and a new week has started for you and your family.

Option #3: To add a more worshipful dimension with regard to ending your Sabbath, read a certain blessing or sing some songs as you enter into the new week with family & friends.

It is wise to be intentional about the time one begins and ends the Sabbath. In so doing, the sacredness of the day will be preserved.

New Testament Connections

When Jews bring the Sabbath to a close they think about all that the new week will bring to them. They believe and acknowledge that Almighty God is in control and as they seek to follow Him and obey Him; He provides salvation. There are many verses in the New Testament that deal with the subject of salvation. Jesus often emphasized salvation in His teaching. An example of this is when Jesus spoke with a Samaritan woman and they discussed the coming Messiah. During this conversation Jesus said to the woman:

> *You worship that which you do not know; we worship that which we know, for salvation is from the Jews. But an hour is coming, and now is, when the true worshipers shall worship the Father in spirit and truth; for such people the Father seeks to be His worshipers. God is spirit, and those who worship Him must worship in spirit and truth. (John 4:22-24)*

Jesus was clarifying to this woman that salvation would come from the Jewish people through the Messiah. He was also explaining to her about our spiritual Father in heaven, God, and how He desires to be worshipped. Salvation is only found in worshipping God the way in which He chooses, not the way man chooses.

As you leave your Sabbath behind and go into a new week with your family it is wise to consider that which our Father in heaven desires from us. Follow after God and trust in Him for all of your needs as you enjoy your Sabbath rest and as you continue throughout the work week.

Chapter 13

Protecting Your Sabbath

I passed by the field of the sluggard,
And by the vineyard of the man lacking sense;
And behold, it was completely overgrown with thistles,
Its surface was covered with nettles,
And its stone wall was broken down.
(Proverbs 24:30-31)

There are times in life when everything we do revolves around a certain event. When a wedding is approaching, the bride and groom begin to make their plans. They set a date and make all the arrangements. Everything revolves around the wedding plans and, as much as possible, nothing else interferes. The wedding takes precedence and everything else becomes secondary. As the bride and groom include others in their plans, family and friends begin to take on a similar commitment to this event. As a result, everyone involved avoids other events that would take them away from the wedding plans.

In the United States people generally commit to attending a wedding at least two weeks prior to the event so that the bride and groom are able to make the necessary arrangements. If there was no commitment to the wedding celebration and people just showed up if they felt like it, this could bring chaos to the celebration and great headache to the bride and groom. The wedding day including all of its aspects must be protected.

This is a similar analogy to the Sabbath day. If the Sabbath day is only regarded like any other day with some different practices, then it will eventually lose its meaning. It must be protected for you as an individual, as a family, and as a community. Many people do not like this concept of protecting the Sabbath because they think it is legalistic or "super religious." For those of you who think this way, I want to put this in perspective.

We as human beings in the twenty first century give priority to our jobs; to the days we work and to the hours that we labor. Our jobs often keep us at work beyond the normal hours and we think nothing of it. There are Sunday afternoon football games or the Monday night basketball games on the television and we think nothing of keeping that appointment every week at the same hour. There are community sports for the children and high school athletic events that can be held any time during the week or on the weekend. Perhaps we go to the gym and work out every morning before work or every evening after work. Maybe you attend an aerobics class Tuesday and Thursday mornings and you have been doing so for several years. Perhaps you have a scheduled card game like Poker or Texas Hold'em every Friday evening. There are a million and one things that we can easily commit ourselves to in a habitual way. However, for some strange reason we think it is odd to give preference to a day of rest, one of the things God has modeled for us in the creation account.

An Israeli friend, whom I will call Eli, was telling me of his six months abroad when he worked in Scotland. During his time there he found himself working seven days a week and completely exhausted. He finally had to go to his boss and ask if he could have his Sabbath back, a day off once a week. At first his boss argued with him saying, "I thought you came here to work!" But eventually he understood and granted Eli's request. Eli, although not a religious Jew, realized that he needed this day off once a week and that he had to protect it.

Steps to Protecting Your Day of Rest

1) Choose your day and hold firm to it (within reason)

I have found that wherever I go, whether in the USA or abroad, I always have to protect my Sabbath. As I mentioned in a previous chapter, when I taught English in Istanbul I generally had to work the weekends and made Mondays my day of rest. Thankfully, the school where I was teaching was closed on Mondays, but I still had to protect my day of rest. I had students that wanted private lessons and friends that wanted to meet on that day. With the exception of unavoidable circumstances, I would not allow anything to interfere with my day of rest.

For those of you with families or living in community, choosing a day that seems to work best for everyone will not be easy. Whenever I stay with families that have children and participate in their schedule, I am overwhelmed with the amount of activity that goes on. There is always something to do every single day. It will definitely be more challenging for those of you in this situation to choose a day of rest. Nevertheless, I recommend that as a family or community you choose the day that works best taking into consideration everyone's individual needs. There will be times when it will be necessary to choose another day of the week because of schedule changes. Perhaps someone will not be able to be with the family or community one Sabbath because of another commitment. The world we live in is not perfect but the goal is to have something as consistent as possible.

2) Strive for Unity

Another important aspect affecting the protection of the Sabbath is the unity between a husband and a wife and the commitment to make the Sabbath a reality. If one of the spouses is disinterested in this whole concept, the Sabbath will become a burden to endure rather than a pleasure to enjoy. Husbands and wives, I implore you to work at this together in order to achieve a workable Sabbath in your home with your family.

For those living in another type of community situation, this same principle of unity is still valid. Those who are trying to keep a weekly Sabbath must be in agreement with each other on certain core issues. Strive to make a workable Sabbath day covenant that will enable all to enjoy this day of rest.

3) Learn to say "No!"

Saying "No!" is simple to say but often hard to put into practice, especially if one is an extrovert or simply enjoys working. However, in order to have a successful day of rest with your family or community, it will be imperative to decline to participate in anything that will take away from your day of rest. This is the case no matter how urgent an invitation may seem. The Sabbath lifestyle goes against the culture in which we live no matter where we live. I continue to struggle to say no to things even in Israel on the Sabbath, because there are even activities here that would distract me from my observance. No matter where one lives, we must learn to say "*No*" to anything that threatens to interfere with our observances of that special day, as much as we are able.

I remember a time when I was attending college and playing tennis for the college tennis team. We generally had practices in the afternoon and games on weekday evenings or on Saturdays. At that time in my life Sunday was my day of rest.

One day a match had been cancelled during the week because of bad weather and it was rescheduled for a Sunday. I struggled with whether to participate in the tennis match or not and debated this decision in my mind. Finally, I decided that it was better to let someone else play in my place and guard my day of rest. Rest was more important to me than a tennis match.

We work and busy ourselves six days a week, live responsible lives, and then put everything aside for one day. We give thanks to God for all of the wonderful blessings in our life and trust Him for the things we still need rather than striving seven days a week. What might you need to say "NO" to in order to protect your day of rest?

4) Limits for Electronic Usage

I know I will be stepping on some toes here and, for that very reason it is probably one of the most important issues. Electronics are with us at every turn in life. Outside of the basics: TV, DVD player, Radio, CD player, cell phones, etc… there are MP3 players, iPods, iPhones, laptops, and Blackberries for internet access and connectivity. We can be plugged in, connected, and online 24/7 if we want to be. Some of us like being able to send an email whenever we want, listen to one of our 10,000 songs at the touch of a button, or get the latest news on our cell phones. Is it possible to lay it all aside for a day?

I am not writing this book to try to be your conscience or to tell you that if you use your laptop on your day of rest then you are breaking one of the Ten Commandments. Each one should evaluate his or her own life before God and determine what is necessary and what is not.

When I stay with my more religious friends in Israel, I try to respect their ways and conform to their way of life while

I am with them. As I have already mentioned, they do not actively use electricity on the Sabbath: i.e. no electronics. I would often have my laptop, cell phone, or iPod with me while I was with them. Sometimes I would sneak the usage of my electronics here and there but eventually I decided that I could do without all of my gadgets for one day. I tried it one Sabbath and found that I did not miss it as much as I thought I would. In fact, I found it quite freeing and have rarely used electronics on my Sabbath since then.

This is one of the beautiful things about the Sabbath day. When we learn to live without certain things that we normally have or use on a daily basis, we learn to appreciate other things that we would not have seen if we had not set those things aside. Electronics are a modern marvel in our generation and they provide many conveniences to us. Which electronic devices, if any, are necessary for you and your family on the Sabbath?

Conclusion:

If you have read to this point something must have resonated within you concerning the Sabbath principle. If the Sabbath is something you wish to practice, you must protect it!

In the book *Fathered By God*, an important truth is explained that I find very relevant with regard to protecting the Sabbath. The author of this book, John Eldredge, includes a chapter titled "Warrior" which explains God as a Warrior. Eldredge reminds men (the primary target in his book) that God is not simply some passive being but rather an active warrior. Eldredge begins this chapter, "Warrior," with a summary of the story of the oppressed Jews shortly after the time of Alexander the Great. He explains how the Jews rose up under the Jewish high priest Mattathias and later under his son, Judah Maccabee, to take back their land and the great Temple in Jerusalem. The celebration of Hanukkah is in remembrance of these events. Eldredge then concludes the opening section of the chapter with this statement:

> *...eventually a man must come to realize that there are certain things in life worth fighting for. Perhaps, when we appreciate the truth of this, we can better understand the heart of God.* [2]

How true these words are! And I believe they are especially true for men as they are called to lead their families. I often find that women, in contrast to men, are more ready to fight for and protect their families. In fact, even in the writing of this book I have come across families where the woman of the home wants to see a Sabbath day of rest implemented into the family schedule but the men are too busy or simply uninterested.

So men, I ask you, what are you fighting for? Are you fighting to protect your family in order to have a weekly day of rest? Men, set your work aside, choose a day of rest (while considering what is best for each member of your family), and enjoy time with your family and with God.

I want to echo these words of Eldredge. I believe there are many good things in life worth fighting for, the Sabbath being one of them. I have been struggling to keep a day of rest in my life for many years and I know that it is not always easy. There have been times when I have held on to it too tightly and damaged some relationships and other times when I have held on to it too loosely and began to forget what it was all about.

What are you fighting for?

Are you fighting for balance in your life and in the life of your family or community or are you simply letting the events of the week dictate your schedule? We fight for that which is most important to us. Our day-timers and calendars will show us what we have made most important in our lives. Sabbath rest, as trivial as it may seem to some people, is one component of life that we must fight for and protect so that we are able to enjoy our lives more fully.

Supplement:

Index of Torah Readings[3]

(The name of each section is generally the first Hebrew word of that text)

Book - Parasha Name	Parsha Portion
***Bereishit* (Genesis)**	
1. Bereishit	Genesis 1:1-6:8
2. Noach	Genesis 6:9-11:32
3. Lech Lecha	Genesis 12:1-17:27
4. Vayeira	Genesis 18:1-22:24
5. Chayei Sarah	Genesis 23:1-25:18
6. Toledot	Genesis 25:19-28:9
7. Vayetze	Genesis 28:10-32:3
8. Vayishlach	Genesis 32:4-36:43
9. Vayeshev	Genesis 37:1-40:23
10. Miketz	Genesis 41:1-44:17
11. Vayigash	Genesis 44:18-47:27
12. Vayechi	Genesis 47:28-50:26
***Shemot* (Exodus)**	
13. Shemot	Exodus 1:1-6:1
14. Va'eira	Exodus 6:2-9:35
15. Bo	Exodus 10:1-13:16
16. Beshalach	Exodus 13:17-17:16
17. Yitro	Exodus 18:1-20:23
18. Mishpatim	Exodus 21:1-24:18
19. Terumah	Exodus 25:1-27:19
20. Tetzaveh	Exodus 27:20-30:10
21. Ki Tisa	Exodus 30:11-34:35
22. Vayakhel	Exodus 35:1-38:20
23. Pekudei	Exodus 38:21-40:38

Vayikra (Leviticus)

24. Vayikra	Leviticus 1:1-5:26
25. Tsav	Leviticus 6:1-8:36
26. Shemini	Leviticus 9:1-11:47
27. Tazria	Leviticus 12:1-13:59
28. Metzora	Leviticus 14:1-15:33
29. Acharei	Leviticus 16:1-18:30
30. Kedoshim	Leviticus 19:1-20:27
31. Emor	Leviticus 21:1-24:23
32. Behar	Leviticus 25:1-26:2
33. Bechukotai	Leviticus 26:3-27:34

Bamidbar (Numbers)

34. Bamidbar	Numbers 1:1-4:20
35. Naso	Numbers 4:21-7:89
36. Behaalotecha	Numbers 8:1-12:16
37. Shlach	Numbers 13:1-15:41
38. Korach	Numbers 16:1-18:32
39. Chukat	Numbers 19:1-22:1
40. Balak	Numbers 22:2-25:9
41. Pinchas	Numbers 25:10-30:1
42. Matot	Numbers 30:2-32:42
43. Masei	Numbers 33:1-36:13

Devarim (Deuteronomy)

44. Devarim	Deut. 1:1-3:22
45. Va-'etchanan	Deut. 3:23-7:11
46. Eikev	Deut. 7:12-11:25
47. Re'eh	Deut. 11:26-16:17
48. Shoftim	Deut. 16:18-21:9
49. Ki Teitzei	Deut. 21:10-25:19
50. Ki Tavo	Deut. 26:1-29:8
51. Nitzavim	Deut. 29:9-30:20
52. Vayelech	Deut. 31:1-30
53. Haazinu	Deut. 32:1-52
54. V'zot HaBerachah	Deut. 33:1-34:12

Notes:

1. Daniel Juster & Russ Resnik, *"One Law Movements: A Challenge to the Messianic Jewish Community."* Published by The Union of Messianic Jewish Congregations. January 28, 2005. p. 6.
2. *"Reprinted by permission. Fathered By God, John Eldredge, 2009, Thomas Nelson Inc. Nashville, Tennessee. All rights reserved."* p. 89.
3. *Wikipedia, the free encyclopedia*: http://en.wikipedia.org/wiki/Weekly_Torah_portion, 5/18/09